11071

THE
IMMORTALITY
OF THE PAST

A. O. DYSON

SCM PRESS LTD

334 00690 2

First published 1974
by SCM Press Ltd
56 Bloomsbury Street London

© SCM Press Ltd 1974

Printed in Great Britain by
Northumberland Press Limited
Gateshead

CONTENTS

PREFACE

'The income of the bequest by the late Bishop Hensley Henson, DD, Hon. Fellow of All Souls College ... to found a lecturership ... shall be applied for the delivery annually ... of not less than four or more than six lectures in the University of Oxford ... upon the subject of "The Appeal to History as an integral part of Christian Apologetics" ' *(Statutes, Decrees and Regulations of the University of Oxford*, 1971, p. 354).

I was elected to deliver the first course of lectures under this foundation in the academic year 1972-3. The lectures are here printed in substantially the form in which they were delivered in the Examination Schools in the Hilary term 1973, but with the addition of notes and references.

I have tried in the first chapter to acknowledge the work of Henson, not only in order to register an act of piety towards the Founder of these lectures, but also to bring before a wider public his own careful reflections on the subject of historical enquiry in relation to theology.

I owe many debts of gratitude: not least to the Very Reverend Henry Chadwick, Dean of Christ Church, Oxford, who first stimulated and then guided my study of Ernst Troeltsch; to colleagues and students, at Ripon Hall over the last ten years, in the Faculty of Theology, and in the Urban Ministry Project, who have in various ways helped me to explore the idea of theological knowledge 'as an advance in the pneumatological knowledge of man and of the world';

to Professor Robert T. Hall of the College of Steubenville, Ohio, for helpful critical comments; to Miss P. M. Ferguson for her typing of the first manuscript; and to my wife, Edwina, for her invaluable help in the reading of proofs.

Ripon Hall, Oxford   *Anthony Dyson*

I

HENSON AND HISTORY

IN HIS essay on 'History and Dogma' Maurice Blondel
wrote: 'One can do nothing without history and nothing
against it.'[1] This dictum points to the dilemma and the
challenge from which the theologian, be he ever so dex-
terous, can never finally escape. It also points to the complexity of the theologian's task. For history is an infinitely
variable phenomenon continually provoking the theologian,
as both the product and interpreter of that history, to new
responsibilities and fresh initiatives. And so, in the history
of ideas, there is scarcely a theme more vexing and more
tangled than the ever-changing relationship between
theology and history. It is a theme which is as old as the
Bible, which has been debated in one form or another in
most eras of Christendom, and which today engages a
remarkable measure of scholarly attention.

At times students of history and theologians have laboured
in amicable co-operation. At other times they have stood in
open conflict. At times theologians have waited on tenter-
hooks for the latest deliverances of historians. At other
times they have derided historical study as irrational and
dilettante. At times historians have turned to theology as
an ally in their constructive task. At other times they have
accused theology of being the servant of superstition and
ideology. At times theologians have incorporated worldly
history into ambitious schemes of salvation. At other times
they have treated historical science as the principal foe of

the Christian gospel. At times theologians have claimed to be the true interpreters of history. At other times they have deserted history in favour of grand alliances with metaphysics. But again and again, by choice or under duress, theology has returned to its preoccupation with the past. More and more, theology has been required to consider its historical bases, its historical claims, its contemporary self-understanding, within a critical study of the past. Are there now, however, signs that the end of an era is at hand? Is the past, as the common possession of theology and history, losing its hold upon human consciousness in a way that has never happened before? Is the very success of historical science not only undermining its own existence and social significance, but also eclipsing that special and decisive past out of which Christian belief has traditionally lived and had its being?

In his 1968 Saposnekow lectures, published as *The Death of the Past*, J. H. Plumb has argued that 'the critical historical process has helped to weaken the past, for by its very nature it dissolves those simple, structural generalizations by which our forefathers interpreted the purpose of life in historical terms'.[2] Plumb asserts that 'in some aspects of life the domination of the past has disappeared almost completely'.[3] 'The strength of the past in all aspects of life is far, far weaker than it was a generation ago; indeed, few societies have ever had a past in such a galloping dissolution as this.'[4] Again Plumb writes: 'History, which is so deeply concerned with the past, has, in a sense, helped to destroy it as a social force, as a synthesizing and comprehensive statement of human destiny.'[5] What are the consequences of this phenomenon? 'As the past dies, and its hand grows palsied in its grip on religion, morality, education, there is a danger of social incoherence, of an idealization of analytic understanding rather than creative belief.'[6] On this view, 'life is change, uncertainty, and only the present can have validity and that, maybe, not for long. The consequence, of course, is to accept a similar attitude in ideas of conduct, in the concepts of social structure or family life. They can be judged by what they do, but lack validity because they have been. So we are witnessing the dissolution of the conditions which tied man to his past and gave him his Janus face.'[7] And so, in summary, Plumb can say : 'Where-ever we look, in all areas of social and personal life, the hold of the past is weakening. Rituals, myths, the need for personal roots in time are so much less strong than they were a mere hundred or even fifty years ago. In education and economic activity the past has ceased to be a guide to the present, even if bits of it still litter and hamper the development of both. In family and sexual relations the past offers little understanding and no comfort. Of course, there are areas of resistance, but they are islands of conviction in a surging sea of doubt. In these aspects, at least, if the past is not dead, the rattle of death can be heard.'[8]

On this view the past is dead or dying. Only the sense of the present remains. But Plumb asserts that the death of the past comes about not only through the zeal and successes of historians; it is also a product of the 'new methods, new processes, new forms of living of scientific and industrial society'.[9] But these new features draw attention to a factor of the present situation which may well be even more decisive in shaping human consciousness than the galloping dissolution of the past. I refer to the discovery of the future. I have in mind, not the many utopias and schemes of universal history which abound in human thought, but rather the way in which the relatively close, this-worldly future has begun to exercise a determinative influence over the present. This is not simply an extension of man's awareness that he belongs to an evolutionary process. For that awareness defines him as a product of the past. On the contrary, the discovery of the future implies a power of human creativity in and over against the present. For some decades, more and more human beings have become aware that mankind now possesses the possibility of radically different futures, each of which is in some measure causally dependent upon contemporary choices in thought, values and planning. Moreover, this pull from the future is not only intellectual in character. It gains psychological roots from the sense of urgency it imposes about the decisions which must be made. As Roger Revelle has aptly remarked: 'We are indeed in a race with time and time is not on our side.'[10] So, because on the one hand rapid change and discovery have broken man's sense of intimate and organic relationship with the past, and because on the other hand the shaping of the future will more and more affect the way in which the present is justified, we can envisage an increasing tendency to understand the present not so much in relation to a known past, not only in its own terms, but from the constraints of alternative futures.

It is not my concern at present to argue for or against the propriety of such an attitude. But if, as there is a growing body of evidence to suggest, this attitude becomes the personally experienced possession of many people, then a very radical shift in cultural self-understanding will have taken place. Such a shift threatens to throw into disarray the traditional functions of, and relationships between, history and theology. May the shift become so decisive that the practice of Christian theology must change, not only in style and emphasis, but in its entire self-understanding? Will theology be obliged, finally and irrevocably, to sever itself from the witness of the past? Will there remain a significant social function for the historian which can serve the theologian's cause? Admittedly these are tentative questions arising from the profound cultural changes whose outline can at present only be dimly discerned and whose consequences can at present only be guessed. But if theology is sensitively to anticipate changing cultural consciousness and thoughtfully to measure its response to such changes, such questions may not be brushed aside. I propose to argue that, against the background of a dying past and an insistent future, the old questions of the relationship between theology and history must be examined afresh. So, in these lectures I shall ask: what is involved for the theologian in the 'appeal to history' and what may now be the force or fate of such an appeal?

In the remainder of this chapter I shall consider how Hensley Henson faced up to what he called the 'formidable responsibilities' attaching to the character of Christianity as a historical religion. In chapter II I shall show how Ernst Troeltsch diagnosed and sought to master theologically that historical crisis whose outlines Henson had perceived. In chapter III I shall explore some features of Rudolf Bultmann's work as exemplifying a radical and influential response from theology to the historical dilemma. In chapter IV I shall ask about the way in which recent studies in the analytical philosophy of history may relate to some of these theological considerations. Finally, in chapter V, I shall return to the question of theology's dual responsibility, *both* towards a world in rapid process more and more under the pull of the future, *and* towards the characteristic message of its historical gospel.

In devoting the rest of this chapter to Henson I am concerned both to recall the memory of the founder of this lecturership and to set him forth as a sensitive and notable guardian of theology's historical conscience.[11] I shall therefore only engage in as much biographical comment as is necessary to document this particular role. A full and definitive biography of Henson has yet to be written. The powers of a future biographer will be severely tested, since Henson lived a many-sided and far from unimportant life. From his earliest days as an Oxford graduate to the end of a long and distinguished life he was engaged in ecclesiastical controversy. For many people his principal claim to fame, if that it be, will lie in this sphere. The more discerning will, however, point to Henson's occupancy of the sees of Hereford and of Durham during which his most characteristic gifts of conscientiousness, honesty and pastoral care were at their most visible and their most effective. Others will with justification point to his remarkable reputation as a preacher and an orator. Thus the lasting contribution of his life to church and nation is hard to estimate. I should judge that it probably lay in his non-conforming attitude of mind and spirit by virtue of which he exercised a prophetic ministry in respect of the dominant intellectual and ecclesiastical fashions of his time. It is, however, as a scholar that Henson will probably *least* be remembered. Yet here, in my view, was the principal source of that prophetic quality to which I have referred. In some respects the title of scholar may seem inappropriate. Certainly Henson left no permanent mark in the worlds of theological or historical scholarship. But he was a person of acute critical intelligence and judgment, well-formed in history and theology, rendered alert in his mental life by a lifetime's habit of careful and intensive reading. It would be a mistake to consent at all readily to Henson's repeated belittlement of his own achievements in the intellectual sphere. On the contrary, it is a matter of surprise that he achieved what he did in this respect when we ponder the constraints of his public life.

Born in 1863, Henson went up to Oxford from Broadstairs School and Brigg Grammar School. He matriculated on 15 October 1881 as an unattached student. In 1884 he was placed in the first class of the School of Modern History. In the autumn of the same year he was elected to a Fellowship at All Souls. Until 1887 he lived in All Souls, teaching history for Trinity College, and for Oriel College, where he was a member of the Senior Common Room. Henson was ordained in 1887. After a temporary post at Anderly and an appointment at Barking, he was re-elected in 1895 to his All Souls Fellowship, living in college on weekdays and ministering at weekends in the chaplaincy of the ancient hospital of St Mary and St Thomas of Canterbury at Ilford. In 1901 he became a Canon of Westminster, a post to which he surprisingly returned, on Churchill's appointment, a year after his retirement. The forty in-between years of his 'unimportant life', as Dean of Durham, Bishop of Hereford and Bishop of Durham, left little space for sustained scholarship. Yet in 1908 Asquith offered Henson the Regius Professorship of Ecclesiastical History at Oxford. The theological waters there were somewhat stagnant, the Prime Minister said, and 'it is time that they should be moved'. Not without soul-searching Henson declined the offer. He had, he admitted, 'some aptitude for teaching', was 'deeply interested in ecclesiastical history' and was 'devoted to Oxford'. But he insisted that the 'literary and pictorial historian has been replaced by the patient and infinitely laborious researcher'.[12] Henson was clear that he could not fulfil this new role. In fact most of his historical writings are short, occasional and often popular in style – based on sermons and addresses. Notwithstanding, Henson remained a keen student of history throughout his life and developed a lively historical sensibility which was always at the service of his ready pen and enquiring mind. Thus Henson's intellectual grounding was primarily historical in character.

A similar story can be told of Henson's theological development. He did not formally read theology at Oxford, perhaps through some anxiety about not repeating the first class of his History Schools! Informally, however, he studied theology with diligence under distinguished tutors and lecturers. Again he produced little substantial work except his book on the apostolic church (which had begun life as part of his submission for the degree of Bachelor of Divinity at Oxford) and his Gifford Lectures on *Christian Morality*, which were conceived and begotten under severe limitations of time and energy. His autobiography and published letters reveal, however, the width and insight of his reading in theology. Thus his historical and theological study

combined to make him a skilled seismographer at a time
of notable change and uncertainty in intellectual and theological life.

From the earliest to the latest of Henson's writings the
phrase 'appeal to history' (or something similar) occurs
repeatedly. Only at the end of his life, however, did the
opportunity arrive for him to explore the theme in a systematic way. Henson had left Durham in January 1939
after nearly twenty years of a 'great and generous episco-
pate'. Some six months later he received an invitation to
deliver the Warburton Lectures at Lincoln's Inn.[13] Henson's
diary records that only a few days later he was giving careful thought to his proposed subject-matter. By September
1939 he was ready to advise the Trustees of his chosen
theme – 'Christian Apologetic the Appeal to History'. The
first lecture was delivered in Lincoln's Inn Chapel in March
1940 and the second lecture in May of the same year. In
October Henson was to learn that the course of lectures
had been suspended owing to the damage done to Lincoln's
Inn by enemy action. In March 1941 Henson was still at
work on the lectures. He had completed the third; but three
remained to be written. But by January 1942, when the
Council of Lincoln's Inn was ready to resume the lectures,
Henson appealed to be relieved of his remaining obligation.
He had, he said, laid aside the preparation of the lectures,
thinking that they could not be resumed until the end of the
war, and had thus begun (and hoped to complete despite failing eyesight) the compilation of the *Retrospect*. The
Trustees generously agreed to his request.

The text of the three lectures which Henson had completed is not, apparently, extant. We have to rely on the
Retrospect and the *Letters* for guidance as to their subject-
matter. After an introductory lecture, Henson dealt with
'the appeal to history against the Jews' and then with 'the
appeal to history against the Gentiles'. He had projected
three other lectures on the appeal to history against the

Christian tradition, against the Papacy and against secu-
larism. In an entry of the *Retrospect* dated 16 October 1940,
Henson explains what is involved in this appeal to history.
In this passage he expresses the view, developed more fully
elsewhere, that historical judgment plays a determinative
role in respect of the claims of Christianity. 'History is not
only the registry of events, but their most authoritative
interpreter, all the more authoritative for being always in
some measure provisional in its verdicts. It is a Court of
Appeal, which is always ready to re-hear a case, if fresh
evidence can be produced. Thus it is not only the great
exegete of what has been, but also the great critic of what
has been thought. The Appeal to History, therefore, is two-
fold. It insists on the relevant facts, and disallows the dominant fiction. It revises the established judgments in defer-
ence to the material which History provides in response to
that Appeal. Thus it has come about that the Appeal to
History has had a great place in the internal development
of Christianity. It has been made both by those who have
resisted innovations; and by those who have advocated
innovation.'[14] It is in the treatment of this 'appeal to history'
that we can locate what I earlier described as Henson's
guardianship of theology's historical conscience. The passage which I have quoted captures the ambiguity of this
'appeal', an ambiguity perceived only too clearly by Henson,
whom a successor in the see of Durham has described as
'penetratingly honest, devastatingly candid, and thoroughly
coherent in this theology, and one of the giants of intellectual liberalism'.[15]

In one respect Henson regards the 'appeal to history' as
a recourse to that sound historical scholarship by means of
which we may distinguish between historical fantasies and
the way things really were. He writes, for example, of the
Roman Catholic Church's 'serenely impudent indifference
to "history"',[16] and quotes with evident disdain Manning's
dictum that 'the appeal to history is itself a heresy'. So too

he regards Christopher Dawson's *Progress and Religion* as
a betrayal of the appeal to history, since the Roman Catholic
church of the Middle Ages was not in fact the kind of
society which Dawson exalts.[17] Again, Henson can say that
'what History has done for the Papacy, criticism has done
for the Fundamentalist Protestant ... In the light of History
the Papal claims are seen to be preposterous.'[18] Here Henson
wishes to assert that the historical evidence will not bear the
weight of the claims which have been made about the
papacy, and that those claims are therefore without foundation.

But in a passage from 1887, just prior to his ordination,
Henson employs the appeal to history in another sense
when dealing with sacraments and church order.[19] The
outline of the argument is as follows: On the traditional
view non-catholics have no sacraments and thus no special
grace: therefore they are morally inferior to catholics: but
this is palpably not so: therefore either the sacraments do
not convey special grace or non-catholics do have the sacraments as well: but we know that the sacraments do convey
special grace: therefore non-catholics do possess the sacraments: therefore the catholic priesthood is no necessary
attribute of a church. Henson concludes: 'Why should we
learn from history for four centuries and then abandon our
teacher? History today has also her lessons.' Here the appeal
to history causes us to revise earlier theological judgments.
Exactly this theme is taken up again some thirty years
later in a note drafted by Henson for Archbishop Lang at
the 1920 Lambeth Conference. 'History is continuously
revising the definition of the Catholic Church.'[20] Here
Henson paraphrases the 'teaching of history' as 'the mind
of the Spirit disclosed in Christian experience'. Thus, according to Henson, we can appeal to the past in order to
criticize contemporary Christian claims based on a false
exegesis of history; we can also appeal to the witness of
history in order to justify our modification of beliefs in-

herited from the past. It is clear that in the first case Henson
envisages an appeal to history in terms of the provisional
deliverances of historical scholarship. In the second case,
however, the appeal to history is different. It is an appeal
to that which Christian conscience feels constrained to
accept as binding (whatever the past may say) on the basis
of the experience of the Christian community in history.
Undoubtedly the second form of the appeal is much less
precise than the first, much more open to dispute. For who
will judge exactly the witness of Christian experience? We
shall see, however, that Henson combines the two forms
in an interesting way.

Now Henson was fully aware that the notion of an appeal
to history had many implications for the New Testament
and, in particular, for the person of Christ. He was adamant
that historical questions may not be by-passed when doctrinal issues are being treated. He writes with scant regard of
those 'who think it sufficient to meet the "obstinate ques-
tionings" of the historian, the critic, and the man of science,
with the *chose jugée* of ecclesiastical decisions'.[21] How then
did Henson approach the historical criticism of the gospels
which he encountered? Writing of his student days in
Oxford, Henson said: 'Mainly I was concerned with ecclesiastical history and the newer study of Biblical science. I
began to understand the method, range, fascination, and
formidable possibilities of criticism ... I learned enough to
follow with intelligence, if not with acceptance, the arguments of both.'[22] Again in his 'Open Letter to a Young
Padre', Henson could say that biblical criticism 'compelled
me to see simple discipleship to the Historic Jesus in the
light of modern theories about Him, and to revise the
opinions which I had hitherto hardly examined on the
crucial question of Biblical inspiration'.[23] For the mature
Henson, this early encounter with biblical criticism was to
crystallize into certain definite opinions. He was clear that,
whatever other resources Christology might employ for its

reflection upon Jesus, it must first and foremost concern
itself with those historical claims which the historian had
judged reliable. Thus: 'Until history has delivered its ver-
dict on the "Jesus of History" Christian Theology (Christology) does not possess the materials for the achievement of
its indispensable task. Only when the historical facts are
known can their spiritual significance be fairly appraised.'[24]
Again: 'I have ever contended, and do still contend, that an
historical fact is a fact certified to be such by adequate historical testimony.'[25] And again: 'To my mind Theology cannot *begin* its work until history has provided so much of
its material as is properly called "historical".'[26] And again:
'Christianity is an historical religion, and it cannot escape
from the formidable responsibilities attaching to that character.'[27]

Clear as these statements are, it is less clear how Henson's
general position worked out in practice. Henson is quite sure
that there is a real vulnerability for theology arising from
the historian's work. But what kind of results in regard to
the New Testament does Henson expect from the historian?
For example, he asserts that 'if historical science should
ever decisively disallow the necessary assumptions of the
Christian Revelation, e.g. by disproving the existence of
Jesus, or by proving his moral inadequacy, then I think the
position of educated Christians would be indeed desperate'.[28]
Are, however, the historian's judgments separable from
theological convictions? Henson believes that they are and
that furthermore they provide the starting-point from which
theological reflection must begin. But the historian is concerned with more than chronology and topography. This
becomes clear from Henson's interpretation of the phrase
'Christianity as an historical religion'. Henson takes this
to mean that Christianity is 'dependent for its truth and
power on the personal excellence of its Founder'. Its
founder, Christ, is the 'true and perfect exponent of God'.
His life and character, as well as his teaching, constitute the

revelation which he made to mankind. The core of this revelation is found in a slender collection of ancient documents which present many problems. To solve these problems we need an understanding of the documents which comes from the practice of historical criticism. 'Human experience knows no other instrument so trustworthy.'[29] Thus Henson writes that: 'It cannot be too often insisted on that the preliminary condition of sound theological thinking is a just interpretation of the documents, and that a just interpretation of the documents implies not only what is called the lower criticism ... but also the higher criticism.'[30] This historical criticism, especially as applied to the synoptic gospels, leads to the establishment of certain facts. These facts are related to doctrine in the following way. If the New Testament facts do not bear out the subsequent doctrine of the church, then the doctrine cannot claim acceptance. We must therefore ask whether there is anything in the facts of the life of Christ which disallows the Christian doctrine about him, or disallows the doctrine and practice of the church. For 'what we believe about Christ can never reasonably be allowed to *contradict* the facts of His history as these are conveyed to us in the documents, justly examined'.[31] On the other hand, if 'a free and impartial examination of the documents justifies *so far as it goes* the doctrine of the Church, then the Church has so far established its case'.[32] Henson wants to emphasize that the New Testament cannot, impartially examined, demonstrate Christian belief about Christ. This belief has a 'profounder and more complex origin'; it will necessarily transcend 'the meagre knowledge which from the documents alone we can gain'. So in the first place the appeal to history means an appeal to the factuality of the picture of the life, character and teaching of Christ as contained in the New Testament documents and as tested by historical criticism. But there must also be another kind of appeal to history.

Henson admits that theology does not proceed only with

assumptions drawn from the results of historical science. Though since the historical facts are always primary, it follows that a strict control is thereby exercised upon the type and range of these other assumptions. We have seen that for Henson the New Testament documents only go part of the way in establishing Christian belief. For they offer only 'meagre knowledge', and belief has a 'profounder and more complex origin'. Here Henson is appealing to the history of Christian experience. He writes: 'Evidence of Christian history ... can bring out into prominence elements which were obscured, and demonstrate the soundness of inferences which only experience could draw.'[33] And again: 'Surely we are following the guidance of reason as well as yielding to the suggestions of piety, when we accept the experience of Christendom as a trustworthy commentary on the sacred text.'[34] So we may say that the historical witness of Christian experience can enlarge historically upon the evidence of the New Testament as long as this witness does not trespass upon areas unsupported by those facts.

This two-fold historical appeal to the New Testament and to Christian experience is apparent in Henson's treatment of the person of Christ. Henson wishes to argue on strictly historical grounds that the gospels set before us one who is the historic foundation of a stream of salutary inspiration which proceeds through human history. As such, Christ is an absolutely unique person. He then proposes to corroborate this historical claim in two ways. First, he argues that the history of Christianity reveals in the undying influence of Jesus Christ on individuals and in the church an absolutely unique fact. An influence of this kind has been ascribed to no other founder of a religion. Second, throughout the whole course of Christian history 'the element of moral vigour within Christianity, and the principle of moral recovery within the Church have been precisely connected with the Personal influence of Jesus Christ'.[35] So Henson concludes that when we speak of the Christ of history we

mean *both* 'the Christ whose Life and Character are made
known to us in the documents of the New Testament' *and*
'the Christ who has made Himself known in the protracted
and various life of the Christian society'.[36] Henson is thereby affirming that the appeal to the undying influence of
Christ and the appeal to the connection of moral vigour and
moral recovery with his person are as much appeals to historical 'facts' as the appeal to the facts of the New Testament disclosed by historical criticism.

One of the most interesting features of this argument
concerns Henson's handling of the New Testament. Again
and again, Henson reminds us of the inexorable limitations
which attach to the conclusions of historical enquiry. But as
frequently Henson, as an historian, insists that historical
enquiry must be honest and thorough. The theologian has,
however, no alternative but to travel the historian's way,
for 'the New Testament must always be the criterion of
tradition'. The Scriptures are the 'fountain-head'; they provide the 'title-deeds of historic Christianity'; 'in them at last
is finality'.[37] But we have seen earlier than Henson pursued
the logic of his argument to the point of allowing that
Christianity would be in a sorry state if historical criticism
of the New Testament were, at crucial points, to yield negative results. How then can Henson be so sure that 'in the
case of the Founder of Christianity a very high degree of
(historical) certitude may be reached by a careful and honest
inquirer'?[38] How do we account for the fact that other
scholars arrive at quite different conclusions?

We have already suggested that much depends on what
the scholar is seeking to establish. Henson claims to seek
historical facts certified, more or less, by evidence. He makes
this point in a rather surprising way. 'The Church offers
first of all the documents of the New Testament, not as
canonical, not as sacred, not as in any sense exempt from
the normal treatment, but simply as historical materials,
the means of forming a reasonable decision on the questions

submitted for examination.'[39] In other words, there is, in the New Testament, material concerning Jesus which may be certified by historical-critical methods as more or less reliable in exactly the way in which we might certify the records relating to any other historical personage. So, of this material we may in the first place ask the straight-forward question: 'Is it reasonable to suppose that Jesus was the kind of person in respect of life, character and teaching that the documents claim?' It is at *this* level, for reasons which I shall discuss later, that Henson claims a deal of historical certitude about Jesus. Now of course even at this level there are many disputed questions among scholars. Towards the end of this lecture I shall consider how such differences affect Henson's approach. But what, in Henson's view, is the link between historical certitude at this level and the more theological claims which are made on the basis of this history?

To understand Henson's method at this point, it is instructive to take two difficult cases – the Virgin Birth and the Resurrection. From this discussion we shall observe the respective weight that Henson gives to historical and theological elements.

Henson asserts that the evidence of the New Testament documents, as handled by the historian, is not of such a kind and quality as to certify the historical fact of a physical resurrection of Jesus. If then the New Testament must always be the criterion of tradition, we must suppose that a theory of the physical resurrection cannot be classified as a doctrine, let alone an essential doctrine. It is what Henson calls a 'pious opinion'. This argument is faithful to Henson's consistent view that the starting-point must always be historical. But we have already noted that Henson has a second mode of appealing to history, namely an appeal to the testimony of the Christian community in history. We also noted that this appeal could in certain circumstances cause us to revise, not our historical judgment of the meagre New Testament evidence, but our conclusions that the inference of a doctrine should be disallowed because of that meagre evidence. Thus Henson must ask whether there is anything in the historical testimony of the experience of the Christian community, in respect of the Virgin Birth and the physical resurrection, which presses us towards such a revision. In a letter to William Sanday, Henson deals with precisely this point in relation to the Virgin Birth.[40] To support a revision of the kind outlined above, Henson would expect to gain (from this second form of appeal) evidence that there is (*a*) some sense that a Virgin Birth is a necessity to effect the Incarnation, (*b*) some measure of 'congruousness' in it and (*c*) some sign that moral and religious interests are properly at stake in this question. If such conditions did, despite the paucity of historical evidence, emerge from the testimony of Christian experience, there would at least be a case for passing beyond agnosticism about the Virgin Birth 'to such a measure of assent as that kind of inferential belief implies'. Henson is clear, however, that the second mode of appeal to history produces no such results. Thus, in respect of the Virgin Birth and the physical resurrection, he must espouse an 'inevitable agnosticism'. The Virgin Birth and the physical resurrection are then, at the least, 'pious opinions' and, at the most, inferences from the 'great and essential doctrines of the Incarnation and the Resurrection'.[41]

How then does Henson's method operate in respect of the (non-physical) resurrection of Christ? His writings on this theme are not entirely clear, but the argument appears to run as follows.[42] The historical evidence of the gospel is not able in principle to demonstrate the fact of such a resurrection. But in its kind and quality it does not disallow inferences to a doctrine of the resurrection. This is the deliverance of the first mode of appeal to history. Employing the second mode of appeal to history we may state that in the Pauline writings and in the history of Christian experience the *conviction* that Christ is experienced as living and present in the midst is a certifiable historical fact. This, according to Henson, provides an adequate basis for the subsequent theological formulation and for the assent of faith which constitute the Resurrection as a doctrine and an article of faith in the full sense. By this procedure we may justifiably assert that the non-physical resurrection of Christ is an 'essential doctrine' in the church. At the same time we must emphasize that for Henson neither the first nor the second modes of appeal can themselves demonstrate a belief. But they can create a situation of legitimate histori-cal probability in relation to which faith and theology may properly proceed without bad conscience.

In considering the background to Henson's approach it is important to recognize that he had lived through the emer-ging movement of source-criticism of the gospels, and that this method had shaped his handling of the text. In later life, however, he had to come to terms with form-critical study. In a letter of February 1935 Henson took an appar-ently cavalier attitude to this new critical tool. 'There is something in form criticism, but nothing that is really new, or greatly important.'[43] But, in fact, in the Gifford Lectures which appeared in print one year later, it is clear that Henson was disposed to take seriously the challenge of form-criticism. He was aware that it was tending to produce very sceptical conclusions about the historical trustworthiness of the gospels. In an entry of the *Retrospect* dated 1934 he speaks of a 'spiritually desolating' form of Bible study and remarks, 'This goes ill with Creed and Worship.'[44] In the Giffords, however, Henson attempts a rational critique of the form-critical method, especially in its hypothesis that much in the gospel tradition is the invention of the early church.

As we have seen, Henson was always cautious about critical study of the Bible, while insisting on its necessity. 'The record of New Testament criticism is filled with the

obituaries of brilliant and widely accepted critical theories.'[45] He admits, however, that as a result of critical study
'many questions remain open, and probably will always
remain so; *yet the fact no wise affects the main lines of
the tradition.*'[46] Henson believes that the gospels are to be
taken seriously as historical documents, whatever theological elements they contain. He contends that a case cannot be proven for asserting that the history of the form of
the tradition discloses a fundamentally unhistorical tendency. The following are typical of Henson's lines of argument.[47]

1. In the stage after its severance from the synagogues,
the church had to instruct Christians as to the practical
requirements of their own religion. 'For this purpose the
teaching and example of the Saviour were of obvious
importance.' The tradition preserved in the synoptic gospels
became their manual.

2. The early preachers depended on the gospels because
they assumed them to be records of fact. Only thus could
the gospels be edifying and authoritative.

3. The belief of the evangelists that their work would
serve their master's cause did not imply any conscious repu-
diation of the historian's normal and recognized obligations.

4. *If* the writer of the prologue to Luke's gospel was the
companion of Paul and the author of Acts, then we have
irresistible proof that the version of Christ's life and teaching
which the New Testament contains was identical with that
which Christ's own contemporaries delivered.

With arguments such as these, Henson concludes that
the form-critical hypothesis about the transmission of
material being undertaken more in the interests of preaching
and faith than of history is exaggerated. There is no rational
ground for assuming that teachers and preachers would
be uninterested in the authenticity of what they taught and
preached. Thus: 'The actual shape in which the Tradition
of Jesus reached the authors of the canonical Gospels does

not appear to be of vital importance so long as we can be assured that the Tradition itself was genuine, and has been honestly handled. Neither point is seriously endangered by form-criticism. When a distinction is made between facts and inferences, the new critical method is less formidable than it looks.'[48] It is noteworthy that Henson does not seek to meet this challenge on dogmatic grounds, but on principles which belong to the historian's science and craft. But that crucial issues of belief were at stake Henson had no doubts. If we had to reject that 'so He taught, so He lived, and so He died', the Christian tradition would indeed run the risk of dissolution.

We have seen that the notion of an 'appeal to history' is understood by Henson in four ways. First, we can appeal to history, i.e. to exact historical scholarship, in order to repudiate readings of the past which are mistaken and misleading. Second, we can appeal to history in order to show forth from the New Testament the life, character and teaching of Jesus. Third, we can appeal to history in order to revise or update theological assertions shown to be inadequate in the light of subsequent Christian experience. Fourth, we can appeal to history, i.e. to Christian life and experience, to corroborate, develop and draw inferences from the meagre knowledge vouchsafed by the New Testament. The first two of these appeals are to 'facts' in restricted sense; the second two to 'facts' in a broader sense. The narrowly historical appeal is always primary. In the light of this analysis I want now to consider some more general implications of Henson's approach to theology and history.

It is of cardinal importance to appreciate what view of theology is presupposed in, and entailed by, Henson's treatment of the appeal to history. For on this there hinges of course the extent to which history may be regarded as a threat to theological science. In Henson's view, theology possesses a tentative character. 'Theology is never more than a provisional correlation of Christian Truth with the rest of human knowledge.'[49] Thus theology is a process of thinking which has three variable components: the results of the first mode of appeal to history in establishing the historical facts about Jesus; the results of the second mode of appeal to history by which the deliverances of Christian experience are determined; and the growth in human knowledge entailing successive, and very different, world-views. But, in addition, Henson holds that theology embraces 'the great presuppositions of Christianity' which are *'altogether independent of the Christian documents'*.[50] That is to say, Christian theology presupposes truths such as the 'lofty theism of the prophets', and the doctrines of divine immanence and immortality whose primary source lies elsewhere than in the New Testament. So we observe that theology is, for Henson, far more than an interpretation of the New Testament, though the New Testament remains its primary criterion since Jesus Christ is the 'true climax and interpretation' of religious and spiritual history. We may therefore expect theology to be a very variable phenomenon, and must beware of ascribing to theological assertions an absolute character which, by their very nature, they cannot possess.

This understanding of the nature of theology relates closely to what may only be called an evolutionary motif in Henson's thought. When we correlate 'Christian truths' with the emerging facts of the duration of pre-human history, the immensity of the universe and the prospect of a lengthy future, we become aware of a need to treat circumspectly that theological understanding which, by comparison, is still local and short-lived. So Henson can speak of the 'petty period of less than nineteen centuries since Christ started this process of spiritual evolution which is to culminate in "the new Heaven and the new Earth wherein dwelleth righteousness"'.[51] There is here implicit a theory of universal history which itself requires correlation both with specifically Christian truths and with the religious quest of mankind. Thus: 'Christianity did not inaugurate the action of the Spirit of God in the affairs of men. It interpreted, exalted, purified, stimulated, and completed whatever in the world was congruous with itself. As in the pre-Christian ages so it is now, and so it shall ever be ... The field of [God's] action is co-existence with creation, and man, as man, is His commissioned prophet.'[52] In this striking passage we observe an instance of that theological responsibility which (in Henson's view) must continually revise and expand Christian truth to take account of our growing understanding of man's place in the universe.

Given this perception of the theological task, we can grasp why Henson could approach the New Testament in the way we have described. Neither the New Testament as a whole, nor the message and life of Jesus enshrined in the gospels, contain all the presuppositions of Christian belief. But they do witness to a living criterion of all prior and subsequent belief and life. We can, and must, turn to other sources in search of material relevant to theology's task. But there is no other source to which we can turn where we will discover a person whose life, character and teaching is the touchstone for all Christian and human phenomena, because that person, Jesus, is the classic exponent of God. Since so much is at stake by way of truth, we may not in the least neglect that criterion as it is witnessed to by the New Testament. For then there would be no control to be exercised upon a wild development of Christian inferences, upon the growth of a stubborn dogmatism which might despise correlation with emerging human knowledge and so lead to superstition, spiritual sloth and religious fanaticism.

Henson's fears in this respect were aroused by a style of theological argument which was becoming popular in his later years – an example of which I shall consider in chapter III. It goes without saying that many of Henson's contemporaries were appalled by what, theologically, he appeared to concede, but equally alarmed that he did not take bolder steps to safeguard what he did not want to concede. For those theologians, historical criticism posed a more serious threat than Henson appeared to allow. For it apparently undermined, or at least called into question, certain claims about God's supernatural activity in Christ and in the world which were far from 'pious opinions', far from 'inferences', but supplied the foundational beliefs of Christianity. Was it therefore possible to defend such claims, in the face of historical criticism, by non-historical means, without giving undue offence to a modern world-view? It will be obvious that Henson was highly sceptical of a programme of this kind since it involved a departure from his own starting-point, namely facts certified as such by due historical enquiry. Consequently, of A. M. Ramsey's book on the Resurrection, Henson asked: 'Does he really understand historical method? Does he imagine that History can be seriously handled under the domination of theological assumptions?'[53] On the same theme Henson took issue with William Temple. Temple, according to Henson, was saying that, if as Christians we postulate that the ruling power in the universe is a person, and that there is a unique revelation, complete and final, given at a moment in history, then we shall expect to find what are usually called miraculous occurrences surrounding that unique event. Henson judges this kind of argument to be 'precarious and even unsound' for two reasons: (*a*) because it may be argued that 'miracle' is incongruous with what we know of God, and because in any case it is all a matter of historical evidence, not of *a priori* assumptions; and (*b*) because, on Temple's view, 'the Christian historian would set about his task of research "with limited liability", *accepting the results of research only so far as they accorded* with the authoritative version of the Sacred History'. 'But,' Henson drily remarks, 'that implies the existence of such a version.'[54] Again, commenting on Rawlinson's *Christ in the Gospels*, Henson asks for more careful consideration of the connection between Christology and history. He observes that 'the conception of "non-historical writing history" eludes me. It ignores the essential issue.'[55] Undoubtedly Henson thinks that initiatives of this kind turn theology on its head. His most precise observation on this theme appears in a letter to Sanday which dates back to 1903. 'It is not the case,' he writes, 'that I forget the influence of the belief in the Incarnation on the credibility of the Gospels, *but I am not clear how far that influence may rightly be permitted to extend*. There are many persons who make that consideration justify a total prohibition of the critical examination of the Gospels. Where are you to stop? So stupendous a fact as the Incarnation makes everything (not morally incongruous) possible; and nothing (however historically incredible) can be properly irrational in that connection. But it is the case that the actual historical circumstances of the Incarnation are only certified to us in testimonies the worth of which must be critically appraised.'[56] Henson recognizes that different types of inference may be made on the basis of the appeal to history, and each type of inference will imply its appropriate weight of assent. But this is quite different from theology making absolute claims about the dogmatic content of the gospel, without serious reference to what is historically given.

It might be argued that Henson's argument is flawed by its insistence upon the need for certifiable historical data about Jesus. If such historical claims are not defensible, then Henson's thesis falls to the ground. Moreover criticism of the gospels has proved more severe since Henson's day. Thus we must either find another basis for Christian faith or allow that it is discredited by such criticism. If we propose to argue along such lines, we must pay careful attention to exactly what Henson is requiring. Prior to *all* theological assumptions, he wants the historians of the gospels to show whether, by the usual procedures of historical science, certain facts are to all intents and purposes reliably reported. Now many historians of the gospels are first and foremost theologians, and we need to determine most carefully whether negative historical judgments are reached by these scholars *qua* historians or *qua* theologians. There is evidence to suggest that those who have come to the gospels as historians have in fact been less sceptical about the basic trustworthiness of the sources than those who have been predisposed in their enquiry by an explicit theological, philosophical or even literary attitude. This is not to deny that the historian has presuppositions. But the basic tendency of his craft, as that of the natural scientist, is always towards the removal of pre-understanding in favour of hypotheses more and more warrantable on historical grounds.

One of the positive features of a position such as Henson's is that it provides within the theological structure a deal of flexibility and a substantial power of responsiveness to changing intellectual and cultural situations. On the one hand Henson takes his primary stand with some fairly general historical data. On the other hand, by affirming that this meagre knowledge cannot provide the full content of faith nor define the whole range of theology, the theologian opens himself to the genuine possibility of correlating Christian truths with growing and changing knowledge. Precisely because the history of the gospels *is* vulnerable, it is a genuine history participating in a wider human history; it is *not* a foreign body in history dictating in an a-historical manner the content of Christian theology *semper ubique*. In principle Henson's position allows the possibility of meeting with some success the challenge to theology provoked by the death of the past and the pull of the future. Henson bids us never to be alarmed if theology turns out very different from what it was in the past; human kind still has a long way to go. But nowhere in any detail did Henson implement the kind of correlation which he had in mind. Did he take seriously the extent to which profound cultural changes might come to undermine those 'Christian truths' which, without fear and with a rare intellectual honesty, he generously put at the disposal of the theologians for free, open and provisional correlation with the facts disclosed by our growing knowledge of man and of the world? However we may go on to answer that question, the fact that it can be posed in those terms marks out Henson as indeed one of the 'giants of intellectual liberalism'.

NOTES

1. Maurice Blondel, *Letters on Apologetics and History and Dogma*, Harvill Press 1964, p.232.
2. J. H. Plumb, *The Death of the Past*, Macmillan 1969, p.14.
3. Plumb, op. cit., p.15.
4. Ibid.
5. Plumb, op. cit., p.136.
6. Plumb, op. cit., p.57.
7. Plumb, op. cit., p.59.
8. Plumb, op. cit., p.60.
9. Plumb, op. cit., p.14.
10. Roger Revelle, 'A Look into the Future', *The Teilhard Review* 5/2, 1970-1, p.95.
11. In this section on Henson I make reference to: *Retrospect of an Unimportant Life*, Oxford University Press, Vol.1, 1942; Vol.2, 1943; Vol.3, 1950; E. F. Braley (ed.), *Letters of Herbert Hensley Henson*, SPCK 1950; E. F. Braley (ed.), *More Letters of Herbert Hensley Henson*, SPCK 1954; *Notes on Popular Rationalism*, Isbister 1904; *Christian Morality*, Oxford University Press 1936; *Apostolic Christianity*, Methuen 1898.
12. *Retrospect*, Vol.1, pp.89-92.
13. *Retrospect*, Vol.3, p.36.
14. *Retrospect*, Vol.3, pp.16of.
15. I. T. Ramsey, *The Modern Churchman* XIII, 1969, p.14.
16. *Retrospect*, Vol.3, p.139.
17. *Retrospect*, Vol.3, p.30.
18. *Retrospect*, Vol.3, p.165.
19. *Retrospect*, Vol.1, pp.21f.
20. *Retrospect*, Vol.2, p.8.
21. *Retrospect*, Vol.1, p.63.

22. *Retrospect*, Vol.1, p.7.
23. *Retrospect*, Vol.3, pp.362f.
24. *Letters*, p.156.
25. *Letters*, p.209.
26. *Letters*, p.169.
27. *More Letters*, p.22.
28. Ibid.
29. *Notes*, p.157.
30. *Notes*, pp.161f.
31. *Notes*, p.167.
32. *Notes*, pp.163f.
33. *Notes*, p.167.
34. *Notes*, p.169.
35. *Notes*, p.210.
36. *Notes*, pp.169f.
37. *Retrospect*, Vol.3, p.362.
38. *Notes*, p.214.
39. *Notes*, p.163.
40. *Retrospect*, Vol.1, pp.71f.
41. *Letters*, p.209.
42. Cf. *Notes*, pp.205-11; *Apostolic Christianity*, pp.94-106.
43. *More Letters*, p.100.
44. *Retrospect*, Vol.2, p.318.
45. *Christian Morality*, p.37.
46. Ibid.
47. See *Christian Morality*, pp.32-64.
48. *Christian Morality*, p.51.
49. *Notes*, p.119.
50. *Notes*, p.164 (my italics).
51. *Notes*, p.112.
52. *Christian Morality*, p.147.
53. *Letters*, p.169.
54. *More Letters*, pp.20f. (my italics).
55. *Letters*, p.156.
56. *Retrospect*, Vol.1, p.71 (my italics).

II

FAITH AND THE HISTORICAL WORLD

WILHELM DILTHEY gave an address on his seventieth birthday. He extolled the revolution in historiography as the liberator of the human spirit from the bonds of natural science and philosophy. 'But,' he asked, 'where are the means of overcoming the anarchy of convictions which threatens to set in?'[1] Some twelve years later in the Auditorium Maximum at Berlin University Troeltsch began his inaugural lecture as Professor of Philosophy and Civilization with the words, 'I have come here to put an end to the anarchy of values.'[2] These two statements capture the background of intellectual conflict and uncertainty in which German theological liberalism waxed and waned.

Henson's treatment of the relations between history and theology embodies many of the strengths and few of the weaknesses of that great tradition of theological liberalism which in Germany virtually came to a halt with the death of Ernst Troeltsch in 1923. Even before his death, the German theological stage was already set for the rise of neo-orthodoxy. Then, from a largely common starting-point, Bultmann and Barth were later to pursue separate but not wholly dissimilar paths, and were profoundly to influence more than one generation of theologians all over the world. The impact of neo-orthodoxy, and of the New Testament studies which were to undergird the Bultmannian school of interpretation, was indirectly experienced by Henson. We have seen in chapter I that he adopted a sceptical and even unbelieving attitude towards their main postulates. But so dominant did neo-orthodoxy and Bultmannian existentialism become for several decades that the earlier, liberal stage of the debate about history and theology was either ignored or forgotten. Yet that earlier debate was no sudden and ephemeral occurrence; it was instead part of a tradition of thought dating back to the late eighteenth century. The neo-orthodox took the view that the route followed by this long tradition had from the outset been signposted as a cul-de-sac. They had therefore no alternative but to break sharply with that tradition, to reforge old theological tools or to forge new ones. Only in the 1950s did the neo-orthodox *volte-face* with liberalism itself encounter any widespread challenge.

All the main questions appropriate to such a challenge were in fact put by Gerhard Ebeling in an essay published in 1950. In Ebeling's masterly analysis the following remarks occur. On the one hand, 'Protestant theology has for the last thirty years been marked by a passionate renunciation of Neo-Protestantism';[3] 'at roughly the same time and in relative independence of each other', Otto, Barth, Holl, Lütgert, Brunner, Gogarten and Bultmann 'threw theology into a ferment'.[4] There was among them 'a wide measure of agreement in their reaction against the nineteenth century'. 'It is a real question, however', Ebeling observes, 'whether the relationship to the nineteenth century does not require to be more carefully considered and reviewed also at *the* very points on which there is today a widespread conviction of having reached a final judgment'.[5] Again, 'the question forces itself ever more clearly upon us, whether the practice of all too quickly dismissing the problems which the theology of the nineteenth century wrestled with is not the increasingly discernible weakness of the theological situation today'.[6] Again, 'the task of even beginning to explore on any wide scale the real theological relevance of the tremendous work of critical historical theology in the nineteenth century is one in which nineteenth-century theology undoubtedly failed and which now, in the general antipathy towards the nineteenth century, threatens to be entirely forgotten'.[7] And again, 'it would be an illusion to hold that this crisis [of the late nineteenth century] with its characteristic historism has been overcome. For all the many anti-historical reactions that have appeared are unserviceable attempts to settle the problem it has brought.'[8]

In this chapter, I propose to review the statement of these historical problems furnished by Troeltsch and to consider the positive directions which he outlined, especially in respect of theology's possible responses to that profound change in cultural self-consciousness which, in his view, lay at the heart of the situation. In this survey I shall bear in mind the total structure of Troeltsch's thought, instead of confining myself to his historical logic as many commentators have done. Such a broader analysis, looking at the range and interconnections of this structure, indicates that the mastery of the historical crisis (for which Troeltsch hoped) involved much more than that accommodation to the spirit of the age with which liberalism has been charged.

The word 'historicism' is a translation of the German 'Historismus'. It had a long and complex history before and after Troeltsch so that his own usage requires careful explanation.[9] Troeltsch used the word in a primary, positive sense and in a secondary, negative sense. In the primary sense Troeltsch means by historicism 'the fundamental historicizing of all our thought about man, his culture and values',[10] or, again, 'the historicizing of all our knowledge and feeling about the mental world'. In the secondary sense Troeltsch speaks of that 'wretched historicism'[11] which leads to scepticism, relativism and the collapse of human values, and which springs for the most part from a 'misapprehended assimilation of history ... to natural science'.[12] Troeltsch argues that this historicizing of thought reached its peak in the nineteenth century, though its roots lie in the period of the Enlightenment. He would concur with Collingwood that, 'the really new element in the thought of today as compared with that of three centuries ago is the rise of history',[13] and with Meinecke that, 'the rise of historicism was ... one of the greatest intellectual revolutions which Western thought has experienced'.[14] On Troeltsch's account the naturalizing of thought in the Renaissance and Enlightenment, disowning the previous authoritative, ecclesiastical culture, spelt a reaction against revelation's claim to unique truth; against the idea of truth being concentrated into a single, divine, redeeming incursion into the world; and against the doctrine of original sin which blocked the appeal to general and necessary truths of reason. So Troeltsch makes three points about what he calls the 'genesis of the modern world'.

1. It is marked by the collapse of a theologically determined culture.[15]

2. It entailed the shattering of a harmonious connection between natural and supernatural knowledge.

3. It meant that nature was rationalized by science to allow incessant new invention and further development.[16] But, according to Troeltsch, early in the Enlightenment this naturalizing of thought gave birth to an excessive rationalism. It is against this tendency that the historicizing of thought emerges at the end of the Enlightenment in men like Herder, then to receive its characteristic stamp from German Idealism and the Romantic Movement. Romanticism in particular introduced a sensibility, a feeling for the unknown and a sense of abandonment to the fullness of historical life, which gave firm support to the growth of modern historical science.[17] Under these impulses, history embraced ever wider horizons. This led to a loss of stable criteria and ushered in the attempt to discover new explanatory categories for which the natural sciences were quick to offer their services in the provision of principles of causality and development. This strait-jacketing of cultural history led to the 'wretched historicism' mentioned above.

Thus the natural world had been opened to independent investigation without reference to, or constraint from, theological categories. The world of cultural history had likewise been released for free investigation. But Troeltsch maintained that this investigation could not proceed in an appropriate way if history had to embrace the positivist methodology of the natural sciences. He therefore set himself the task of developing an autonomous historical method. He regarded Dilthey, however, as the first thinker to state the need for an independent theory of historical knowledge which alone would give historical scholarship a firm basis. Dilthey saw that the positivists were trying to furnish this basis 'by a transference of principles and methods from natural science'.[18] But, Troeltsch asserts, by the labours of Dilthey, Windelband, Rickert, Bergson, Simmel and others 'a path was cleared for an historical logic which disclosed a second world alongside that of nature'.[19] He recognized that the scale and diversity of cultural history was bound to lead to a 'certain degree of relativism', though a thoroughgoing relativism was in no wise inevitable. It was not, however, solely the responsibility of historical science to deal with these problems. As we shall see, Troeltsch turned to metaphysics, to theology and to what can almost be called an 'existentialism' in search of an adequate response to this threatening anarchy of values. In the first place, however, Troeltsch was concerned to elaborate a conceptual foundation for historical science based on 'individuality' and 'development'. I shall first consider the idea of 'individuality'.

Meinecke has written: 'What Western civilization now underwent was perhaps its greatest revolution in thought. For the faith which had hitherto prevailed, that there is in Reason and in its utterances a comprehensible unity and sameness and consequently a universal validity, was shattered and discarded once it was realized that Reason in fact manifests itself in infinitely various forms ... Everything in history now took on a different appearance from before, things no longer lay in the same plane open to uniform scrutiny ... it was no longer the same things which eternally recurred ... but an eternal process of newborn, unique, and incomparable events ... What was now seen was a world entirely full of individuality.'[20] Troeltsch adopts a twofold approach to individuality : a philosophical treatment recalling Schleiermacher; and a historical and hermeneutical treatment recalling Dilthey. But in Troeltsch these two approaches are organically connected.

Troeltsch takes as the basic object of historical science, not the separate event, but the individual totality *(individuelle Totalität)*. The 'totality' refers to a unified segment of life, a given conglomeration of occurrence which imposes itself upon the historian's powers of selection and demarcation. It is a cohesive grouping of historical life discernible in the flow of events. This totality may be a nation, a cultural era, a revolution – but rarely an individual person. Obviously the historian cannot encompass all that belongs to this totality. He must therefore fix on traits which are characteristic of its life. Troeltsch summarizes as follows the advantages which accrue from this individualizing approach to history. 'We are free from the entire naturalistic constraint of that abstraction of general laws which prevails in the natural sciences; free from the atomism which dismembers everything and artificially puts it together again; from the enervating effects of determinism; free from the equivalences which level everything down and from which even the construction of a special spiritual causality cannot save us. Then we become free again for the autonomous living ascription and measurement of value out of our own spontaneous needs; free for the living choice of those elements in history which seem to us pre-eminently suited to such treatment; and free from the weight of that which is for us indifferent or dead. We live again in what is whole, moving and creative, and we understand the responsibility

of the moment and of personal decision. No more do we see
before us a chain of abstract necessities in which only the
particular combination at any one time is new and personal
but where the totality and the essence remain the same.
Rather we see before us an active drama embedded in this
world, which runs its course on the heights of the organic
development of life with all manner of explosions and incal-
culable occurrences ... We are delivered from that wretched
Historismus which was for the greatest part ... a miscom-
prehended assimilation of history by the particular elements,
general laws, sequence-formations and necessities of natural
science ... Life is restored to us. We are no longer suffocated
by its confusions, but can develop the basic principles of
its order and arrangement into scientific rules and principles
of formation. These basic principles of order and arrangement are given with life itself; we can use them instinctively
without thereby losing life itself again.'[21]

In this way Troeltsch exposes the concept of individuality
as pointing to a historical method. But he also wishes to
show that it contains the potential for a world-view. He
is aware of the possible intellectual and moral anarchy
implied in history as a collection of disparate individual
totalities related neither to each other, nor to the present
and future. It would still be a historical atomism, though
an atomism of disparate totalities rather than of separate
events. So it is that out of this concept of individuality
Troeltsch explores the idea of 'development' *(Entwicklung).*
The word 'development' is perhaps misleading to the English
ear, carrying overtones of progress and teleology. Elsewhere
Troeltsch speaks of it as a 'continuous connection of becoming' *(kontinuerlicher Werdezusammenhang),* which is
an unwieldy but more precise description. In the first place,
'development' refers to the life of the individual totality as
movement, process and flow of becoming; it refers to a
single concrete impulse governing a given aggregate of

historical life.[22] But the historian's handling of development within an individual totality will naturally lead him to consider development in respect of two related totalities, or of a group of totalities which encompasses a whole cultural tradition. This is a proper progression since, as a matter of fact, each individual totality is tied in all directions to the flow of phenomena which surround it; the individual totality is a part of 'general historical agitation and fluidity'. Troeltsch speaks of the 'important logical result, that the continuous becoming of historical things, where it is truly continuous, cannot be presented in a purely causal manner by ranging together certain particular events. Rather the particular events are fused together into a developing unity which interweaves them and dissolves them into each other, and which thus makes itself continuous.'[23] But this wider intuition of development follows (it must be insisted) inductively from the perception of the development which belongs to the individual totality.

Troeltsch is acutely aware of the difficulties which confront the historian in the depiction of individuality and development. In view of the gap between the historian and his material, how can we be sure that in principle the characteristic traits of novel and original historical phenomena can be grasped? What is the relationship between historical method and historical reality? Here Troeltsch finds himself forced in the direction of a 'metalogic' in order to make decisively the point that 'individuality' and 'development' are more than constructions of the historian's mind, but rather belong to the deepest inner movements of history. In this regard he explores the fruitfulness of a monadology, drawing upon, and modifying, Leibnitz to suggest that the individual totalities of life which come to us through the mediation of finite spirits are continuous movements in the divine life; and upon Malebranche, for whom the processes of development are not causal principles operating in an empirical series but rather the participation by finite spirits in the inner unity and movement of life of the divine Spirit.[24] The forms which we intuitively discern in history reflect the inner connection of the divine life which encompasses all reality. We are in consequence able to know alien subjectivity because we actually bear it within us in view of our common identity with the divine spirit. Now Troeltsch's excursus into metaphysics should not be misunderstood. Highly critical of metaphysical philosophies of history (such as that of Hegel), Troeltsch uses the monadology as the only means that thought can find of adequately maintaining a just balance in the relationship between the rational and the irrational, between the actual and the logical, between creation and the eternity and necessity of the world. He is only too aware that no neat and final synthesis is possible.

The conceptual foundation of Troeltsch's historical logic, based on individuality and development, has far-reaching consequences. For historicism means that man's fixed external points of reference are removed. He has to establish his own criteria for the fashioning of personal and social life. But this does not have to be an arbitrary procedure, since the criteria for the modification of the present can derive from the value which we ascribe to individual circles of development in the past. How is such value to be grasped and applied? Troeltsch considered, but rejected, Rickert's scheme of *a priori* values on the grounds that they do not really come into contact with historical life. 'History becomes an arsenal of examples for the theory of value.'[25] So, finally, Troeltsch seeks to relate two factors: (1) an inner will and urge to evaluation; and (2) the manifoldness of history, understood in terms of individuality and development, wherein values lie. In this action of the inner will upon history, relating present and past, we execute the cultural synthesis (or material philosophy of history). In turn, from the new standards which derive from this cultural synthesis there eventually emerges a way of life. So the operation of the cultural synthesis points to the belief that it is particular cultural contexts which are expressions both of the divine ground of life, and also of the inner movement of that divine ground towards a total meaning unknown to us.

I have tried to show in general terms that, in the midst of his treatment of historical logic and the theory of value, Troeltsch is concerned to explore the deeper implications of that view of the historical world disclosed by historicism, and in so doing allows his mind to range freely over the kind of theological possibilities which might be congruous with the nature of that historical world. At first sight this historical logic suggests no more than a world of intense flux and endless variety. But we begin to discern that individual totalities have their own value and, through the concept of development, that totalities of history are related to each other, however untidily, by common impulses. We consider how the values of past circles of development can be brought into the present for the new formation of standards. And so we come to ask what sort of total picture of historical reality might emerge, bearing in mind an indefinite future and countless cultural syntheses. Bornhausen rightly observes that at every point Troeltsch's work seems to pose the question: 'Does history conceal an ultimate?'[26] And Troeltsch himself wrote that 'even in the cultural synthesis which the philosophy of history must outline in the contemporary situation, the religious theme remains at the centre'. Again, as early as 1898, Troeltsch suggested that 'one can almost speak of a latent theology of historicism'.[27] But before we consider the ways in which this latent theology might become actual, we must first observe that the conceptual foundations of individuality and development presuppose a thoroughgoing critique of much traditional theology.

In an important early essay entitled *Die wissenschaftliche Lage und ihre Anforderungen an die Theologie*,[28]

Troeltsch asks how the Christian experience of salvation and
the world-view which corresponds to it are now to be
related to facts about the world deriving from modern scientific knowledge. In another early essay he suggests that within this overall challenge, it is historicism which provides the
principal threat to theology, undermining theology's central
claim. This is made clear in the following quotation: 'Supernaturalism was a way of thinking which had closed, inviol-
able, generally-valid, and firmly grounded ideas. Historicism
knows the ideas of all ages, and even its own ideals, as historically conditioned. For this reason it knows of no belief
which could be normative for it.'[29] The debate with Julius
Kaftan makes clear, however, that Troeltsch does not here
have in mind a rejection of supernaturalism as such. Instead
he rejects what he calls 'the supernatural which belongs
only to Christianity', or again 'an entirely idiosyncratic
causality of revelation proper only to Christianity'. Once
we admit the historical method, such exclusivity cannot be
maintained. For example, when this method is applied to
the New Testament, we encounter 'an interweaving of Christian and extra-Christian material, and a dependence upon
the total situation'. Troeltsch continues: 'To be sure, this
does not remove Christianity's autonomy; it rather reveals
it as a phenomenon with extraordinary power of assimilation. But it does render impossible a separation of natural
and supernatural elements, a distinction between what is
humanly conditioned and that which is directly divine.'[30]
In arriving at such a judgment in relation to the New
Testament, Troeltsch was expressing a certain indebtedness
to the work of the history of religions school. But of course
his general point of view here follows directly from his treatment of individuality and development. The history of religions school had simply confirmed and illustrated his thesis
but with special reference to Christian origins. If we treat
early Christianity as an individual totality, then each event
within this totality is horizontally related to, and dependent

upon, others around it. But the individual totality itself is horizontally related to extra-Christian totalities in a larger circle of development. It is therefore impossible for the theologian to conceive of single events of an exclusively supernatural kind, since no one event can be exclusive of another. This was in part a mistaken assimilation by theology of a scientific notion of separate 'elements'. History, on the other hand, does not present us with simple units, but with 'magnitudes which have already coalesced'.[31] Such a theory in no wise excludes novelty from the historical process, but this novelty is never discontinuous with what precedes and surrounds it.

In his essay on historical and dogmatic method in theology,[32] Troeltsch explains in greater detail how historicism is a leaven which transforms everything and finally explodes the whole form of theological method as known hitherto. He contends that dogmatic method has its starting-point outside history whence it derives certain absolute propositions. At this initial and crucial point dogmatic method is supposedly immune from historical criticism. It thus treats as normative certain events or facts which do not belong to ordinary history, cannot be refuted by historical criticism and are guaranteed as to their facticity by appeals to miracle, revelation, faith, etc. On three counts dogmatic method cannot allow these special events or facts to be submitted to historical criticism. First, it could not accept the inevitable conclusion of historical method that their historicity is at best a matter of probability. Second, the historian, in seeking to establish their historicity, would appeal, on the basis of analogy, 'to the normal, usual, or at least widely attested modes of occurrence and circumstances which we know';[33] whereas the theologian is claiming *a priori* that these events are unique. Third, to hand over these events to historical criticism would involve their insertion into the whole network of empirical occurrence with its principle of reciprocal causality; whereas these events are supposed to follow a different, spiritual law of causality. Rejecting such principles, the dogmatic method divides historical reality into two spheres: a sphere free from miracle and open to the usual historical-critical method; and a sphere controlled by the miraculous and only investigable by criteria drawn from categories of inner experience and revelation. On the other hand, 'the historical method leads, by [historical] criticism, analogy and correlation, of its own accord and with irresistible necessity, to the recovery of a reciprocally-conditioned network of expressions of the human spirit – expressions which are at no point absolute or isolated, but rather stand everywhere connected and can, on this view, only be understood in the context of a well-nigh all-encompassing whole'.[34]

We see here that the concept of development is crucial for Troeltsch's rejection of supernaturalism. The argument appears to run as follows: history is to be seen as a stream of historical becoming in which each part is linked to its antecedent and succeeding parts; Christianity belongs to this stream of history; therefore all the events of Christianity belong to, and are interwoven in, this complex network of occurrence. Thus, only if events stood somehow in isolation in history would a theory be defensible which concentrates the divine revelation absolutely and uniquely in certain specific events.

In order to develop in a *positive* direction the latent theology of historicism, Troeltsch had to envisage a science of religion which respected both the restrictions and possibilities of historicism. For Troeltsch, this science of religion embodies an interplay of questions relating to psychology, epistemology, philosophical history and religious metaphysics. At different stages during Troeltsch's intellectual development, first the psychological, then the epistemological, and then the historical component assumes a position of dominance. It is the latest and most mature phase of Troeltsch's thought which concerns us here. He spells out his intentions as follows: 'Thus we are challenged to construct theology on the basis of a historical, even universal-historical method.'[35] This implies the need to develop a 'general systematic exposition of religion on the basis of its history'.[36] This means the attempt to grasp the individual totalities of Christian religious history, to elucidate their characteristic traits and to determine their value. For he is thoroughly opposed to any affirmation of the value of a religion by reference to external criteria. He can therefore answer the question about validity only by actually comparing different religions in their historical manifestations. This is of course an exceptionally difficult task, and we see in Troeltsch a number of attempts to deal with the question of the historical supremacy of Christianity.

In his early essays Troeltsch took the view that Christianity evaluates itself as supreme to the person's own inner experience. But as the historical motif becomes dominant, e.g. in *Die Absolutheit*,[37] this psychological argument is superseded. On the basis of historical comparison Troeltsch asserts that 'the antithesis is in fact one between Prophetic-Christian-Platonic-Stoic religion [and] Buddhistic-Oriental religion. These alone manifest productive power.'[38] But the decision as to which tradition is superior cannot be determined by historical science; it is a matter of personal conviction. Troeltsch himself, at this stage, took the view that Christianity alone has revealed a living Godhead which challenges the soul to sever itself from the world and unite itself to the divine, but which also requires the soul to return to the world and there build up a kingdom based on the infinite value of personality. Of course, in harmony with the canons of historicism, Troeltsch must allow that the future might bring a higher revelation. In practice, the belief that Christianity marks the climax of the historical religion leads him to conclude that it is unsurpassable. But in a later essay, dated 1913, Troeltsch again modifies his view of Christianity's supremacy. He reaffirms that 'in my

own opinion the decision will be reached in favour of pro-
phetic-Christian theism, as over against the quietism and pes-
simism of the oriental religions'. But he qualifies this by
adding that he refers only to the European and American
world. This essay concludes: 'Indeed the very thought of
setting forth any one historical religion as complete and final,
capable of supplanting all others, seems to us to be open to
serious criticism and doubt.'[39] In *Christian Thought* this
restriction of the supremacy of Christianity to an European
and American milieu is made wholly explicit.[40]

In this phase of the discussion we discern in Troeltsch
some unease. He feels inhibited in his comparative work by
the sheer size and diversity of religious-cultural history.
Regarding Christianity, he speaks of 'an extraordinarily
extensive world of thought and life with widely divergent
periods and epochs'.[41] But a mere acceptance of this diversity
is a symptom of 'wretched historicism'. In principle,
Troeltsch ought to be able to symbolize or represent Christianity in its essential trait. Thus he embarks on the quest
of a historical 'essence of Christianity' which belongs to all
or most of its historical manifestations. This essence cannot
of course be deduced from extra-historical sources. Schleiermacher, Harnack and Hegel had all tried to determine this
essence without reference to a-historical supernaturalism,
but none of them adequately took the historical element
into account. Against these efforts Troeltsch writes, 'the
determination of essence is a purely historical task'.[42] The
way in which Troeltsch seeks to disclose this essence reflects
his understanding of the way in which the cultural synthesis must be achieved, and of the way in which thought
and action combine past and present in the formation of
the future. In Harnack, the essence can be contained in a
single static formula. But, Troeltsch insists, 'the essence
differs from epoch to epoch, resulting from the totality of
its influences'. So the essence can only be understood as the
'productive new interpretation and adaptation of historical-

Christian forces corresponding to the total situation at any given time'.[43] The religious thinker approaches the religious past, describing and evaluating totalities, and seeking to relate them to the living issues of the present. 'Through this, progress is accomplished – progress as the further formation of the historical element for the future.'[44] Again Troeltsch can describe the essence as in fact 'the subjective, personal interpretation and synthesis which present thinking derives from the entire situation with reference to actual living issues and for the purpose of directing future activity. Thus there is involved a general, historical feeling and understanding, but also a subjective and creative interpretation and construction.'[45] It follows that the essence will never recur in the same form; it will always change as the total situation changes. Here Troeltsch's argument turns full circle and the primary, positive sense of historicism is made clear. It was, we recall, the problem of the 'profits and losses' resulting from the 'fundamental historicizing of our knowledge and thought, for the formation of a personal intellectual life and for the creation of the new social and political conditions of life.'[46]

Now it is at first sight difficult to impose a sense of order and structure upon Troeltsch's ideas. His work has been described as a series of 'preparatory studies' (*Vorarbeiten*) which defy such organization. But underlying the variety and prolixity of Troeltsch's writings I believe that we can trace a firm intellectual shape and order. From the original premise of the historical revolution, Troeltsch seeks to develop for historical science an appropriate method based on the characteristic nature of cultural history. He then wants to show that herein is implied at two levels the question of a world-view. First, there are the questions as to the relationship between the cultural historian and his material, and as to the contemporary function of the historian. These are questions about value in history. Second, there is the question as to what basic understanding of human and worldly reality is presupposed by this understanding of history. This is a metaphysical question. These two levels of enquiry converge upon the task of the cultural synthesis. Latent in all these questions, and in the cultural synthesis, is a theology which is required by this perception of history. Before Troeltsch can investigate the procedures of such a theology, he must clearly identify the kind of theology which is disallowed by historicism. For historicism shatters a theologically-determined world-view and wholly undermines exclusive supernaturalism. But if we follow the course prescribed for religious history by the canons of historicism, we shall be able to foster a living science of religion which can relate the past to the present in a formative way. Such a theological enterprise lies at the heart of the cultural synthesis; and such a cultural synthesis will always point to a religious metaphysics as referring to the ultimate ground of its contents. The function of theology in Troeltsch's scheme is admirably summarized by Vermeil. 'Theology is a living science which, far from confining us to transmitting the traditional affirmations or to engaging in apologetic, orientates us across the intellectual life of the present, reconstructs the religious idea, and works for the reform of its institutions.'[47]

Now part of the difficulty of evaluating Troeltsch's proposals arises from the fact that he left us no substantive example either of the cultural synthesis in general or of its theological component in particular. This, Troeltsch claimed, was the task to which he would next turn. If that was in fact the case, then death prevented his execution of this task. But we cannot help asking whether he had set himself a task which was in principle too ambitious. To achieve effectively what he intended would have entailed nothing less than a cultural history of the world or at least of the West. It is hard to guess at the character of such a history as material for the cultural synthesis. In one sense this is an important question. For it calls in doubt the validity of

Troeltsch's overall approach. On the other hand such difficulties should not distract us from the enormously suggestive
character of Troeltsch's *Vorarbeiten* in their imaginative
approaches to the historical question. As a result of his work,
Troeltsch presents for consideration certain criteria and
starting-points in relation to the theological enterprise which
deserve attention, whatever may seem to be the fate of his
hopes for a material philosophy of history. It is these criteria
and starting-points which I shall discuss in the remainder of
this chapter and to which I shall return in chapter V.

It was surely evident that far more lay behind Henson's
'appeal to history' than a nervous concern about the historical trustworthiness of the New Testament. For Henson,
history in a wider sense was the final court of appeal both
for and against theological claims. So too the crisis of
historicism to which Troeltsch bore articulate witness
represented far more than an aggressive anti-dogmatic scepticism. It was, we must recall, a crisis for all the human
sciences. It points to a fundamental incompatibility between
a view of man-in-society as autonomous and a view of
human life and activity as governed by metaphysical or
theological laws which, from beyond, control the movement
of history. It is also a clash between that view which takes
with fullest seriousness the extraordinary diversity of
human history, and one which regards human history as
somehow focussing upon, and shaped by, a history of salvation whose decisive moments are miraculously disclosed
in a certain line of human history. The rise of the sciences
in general, and of historical science in particular, disposses-
sed Christian faith of a self-evident validity which it had
possessed for over one thousand years. The tables are so
turned that in the modern age we ascribe self-evident
validity only to that which 'man as such with his rational
and empirical faculties can know, perceive, prove and control'. We have been all too aware in recent theological discussion of the problems created for theology by this kind of

world-view. But, as Troeltsch has made clear, there are
profits as well as losses.

First, although a historicized theology cannot allow for
any *immediate* and *direct* disclosure of divine action or
character in history, it does permit the elaboration of a
doctrine of divine immanence in which the 'other', the
transcendent, is experienced within the movements of historical life. As we reflect upon the values arising from Christian religious history, we encounter what piety can legiti-
mately call the self-revelation of an immanent-transcendent
God, but a revelation which passes through the mesh of
human consciousness and action in a history marked by
individuality and development.

Second, in a way reminiscent of Henson, Troeltsch invites
us to take with great seriousness the theological content of
what is actually produced in history at the human level by
that stream of 'salutary inspiration' which flows from Jesus
in the prophetic tradition to which he belongs. For there are
thus provoked among men new values, new initiatives, new
self-understandings which can shape the warp and weft of
cultural history. These new features come down into our
contemporary history and provide some of the resources by
which we may constructively respond to the contemporary
historical world.

Third, Troeltsch obliges us to face up with realism to the
totality of history as the occasions by which God's purposed
future is significantly realized. Such a view requires us to
inspect with insight and sympathy cultural histories other
than our own, and the religious traditions which have
sprung from those cultures.

Fourth, the character of history disclosed by Troeltsch's
analysis precludes any kind of salvation history which
occurs externally to man's action in society. This is not
to propose that man effects his own salvation, but rather
to suggest that the interplay of divine grace and human
action is hidden within the depths of individual and cor-

porate life in history, so that the resultant actions of man and the movements of culture (which the historian seeks to capture) have to the outward eye an wholly human character. In fact the appearances are only partly true. For though man does shape the future, he does so in the light of convictions, values and hope which spring from the divine purpose as the ground of history. Thus to the theologian's eye, history can be regarded as a hidden dialectical process between divine and human motivation which comes to the surface as that cultural history for which individuality and development are necessary categories. Within such a view, Troeltsch takes full account of the sheer contingency which belongs to history in many respects. On account of this, the dialectical process may *outwardly* evince few signs of progress, development or growth. It is only from religious convictions about God, his immanent activity and his envisaged goal, that we can presuppose progress, growth and development (when it occurs) to be creative movements of a universal-historical process.

Fifth, the programme which Troeltsch has in mind gives greater emphasis to theology, not as a past-centred, but as a present-centred discipline and therefore as a discipline which can respond to the pull of the future. Theology does not so much bring a theological world-view from the past to see how far, by adjustment and restatement, it can be given force for the present. Rather it reflects directly upon issues of the present in the light of the values which the cultural historian brings from the religious past. Thus theology is not primarily an expository discipline. It is a critical and inventive discipline whose subject-matter concerns the quality and content of the personal, intellectual, social and religious life of the present and the directions which it must take for the future. This prescription for the theologian's task accords ill with the traditional view. But, on a pattern similar to that suggested by Henson, Troeltsch would prefer to see the revelation associated with Jesus and his tradition as the presupposition of theology rather than its working content. The revelation has been given in the life, character and teaching of Jesus. Theologically significant is the out-working of that historical revelation in subsequent history, its effects as it is inserted in new cultural movements and traditions. For the historical effects of revelation have a factual character which can be investigated by historical research. The more speculative problems Troeltsch reserves for what he calls religious metaphysics. This discipline does not have a factual character and provides only tentative (but necessary) reflective support for the properly theo-logical task. Theology, on this view, is not hindered in ful-filling its responsibilities by a failure to reach agreed and assured results on these more speculative questions.

Sixth, these considerations suggest why the question about the trustworthiness of the New Testament documents is not of decisive importance to Troeltsch. He says that 'the his-torical task of theology does not merely consist in estab-lishing the degree of historical credibility and authenticity of the biblical writings by a continuous haggling which then makes greater or lesser concessions to "criticism" '.[48] As a matter of fact he took the view that, historically speaking, the main outlines were reliable enough. But the phenomena to which the New Testament documents bear witness have in fact provoked their effects in history and that history is open to inspection and description. Those effects cannot be revised, even if New Testament research should come up with conclusions very different from those which we have known. In this respect Troeltsch differs from Henson. For Henson it is vital that the outlines of Jesus' life, character and teaching be historically reliable, as providing the neces-sary criterion for judgments about the later tradition.

Seventh, in Troeltsch (as in Henson) we can observe an important redisposition of forces within the spectrum of theological activity, and an important shift of emphasis as to where the boundaries should be drawn. Much is given over to the area of faith or piety. Troeltsch in no way minimizes the place and weight of piety. But it *is* always a matter of personal conviction; in a historical world we may not claim that the utterances of piety assume the character of theological 'facts'. Again the emphasis shifts from theological-metaphysical questions to the engagement with living issues of the present. Further, the frontiers within the theological enterprise are not fixed. Troeltsch can allow, for example, that the facts of historical experience can come to shape afresh our religious understanding of reality. This can be seen in the way in which the historicized world of cultural history points away from the notion of a special *Heilsges-chichte* towards the monadology.

Eighth, at one important point Troeltsch suggests that historicism points to a radically different way of viewing reality. We recall that for Troeltsch the unit of historical science is not the separate event but the totality, the circle of development. This represents a sharp critique of what J. N. Findlay has called the 'diremptive' tendency in Western thought. This tendency can be illustrated in countless ways – in the preoccupation of ethics with acts, of physics with the smallest units, of philosophy with words and sentences, of theology with events, and of history with facts. Troeltsch's concern for the *Zusammenhang* reflects changes that are now taking place in other disciplines towards a more relational and systemic view of their subject-matter. *If* Troeltsch's view of cultural history as a continuous network of becoming can be extrapolated to a similar view of created reality in its entirety, then the implications for theology in its view of God and Christ in relation to the world are many and far-reaching.

Ninth, and finally, we observe that this critical reaction to the diremptive tendency in theology allows a far more fruitful encounter with the collectivities of human reality than has often been the norm in Christian theology. It might cause us to look critically (as Stendahl has done in his essay on 'St Paul and the Introspective Conscience of the West')[49] at the individualizing interpretation of the categories of salvation and justification, and so explore a more satisfactory basis for a theology and an ethics in which individual and collective are in balanced interplay.

In the period following Troeltsch, many theologians have consciously or unconsciously rejected the challenges to theology implied by historicism. They have returned to modes of thought and to theological programmes expressly ruled out of court by the conditions and constraints which Troeltsch regarded as henceforth binding. Has this arisen because his proposals are impractical or mistaken, or because the long-standing theological tradition of the West has not yet come to terms with the irreversible tendencies set in motion by the fundamental historicizing of our world? Or is this return to former ways dictated by a fear of losing what is most stable and significant in the Christian message to which theology has borne witness? In the next chapter I shall consider the response of a theologian who proposes to maintain a much firmer grasp on the tradition of exclusive supernaturalism than Troeltsch would have deemed possible, but who at the same time is concerned to acknowledge the challenge of modernity in other respects. Is this a symptom of desperate rearguard action or a legitimate and powerful rejoinder to Troeltsch at the most sensitive and vital point? For there is little doubt that Troeltsch admits of no light dismissal. 'He perceived,' as Drescher has written, 'like no other theologian of his time, the upsetting and urgent features of the relation between faith and history. No one else posed such profound and serious questions about the significance of the historical method for theology ... The rise of dialectical theology and the outbreak of the Church Struggle suppressed these and other problems bequeathed by liberal theology, but by no means dealt with them.'[50]

NOTES

1. W. Dilthey, *Gesammelte Schriften*, Vol.5, Leipzig and Berlin 1923f., pp.7-9.
2. L. Marcuse, *Mein zwanzigstes Jahrhundert: Auf dem Weg zu einer Autobiographie*, Munich 1960, pp.49ff.
3. G. Ebeling, *Word and Faith*, SCM Press 1963, p.17.
4. Ebeling, op. cit., p.23.
5. Ebeling, op. cit., p.24.
6. Ibid.
7. Ebeling, op. cit., p.59.
8. Ebeling, op. cit., p.48.
9. I have examined in detail the history and uses of this word in my Oxford doctoral thesis *History in the Philosophy and Theology of Ernst Troeltsch* (1968), chapter 2.
10. Troeltsch, *Gesammelte Schriften*, Vol.3, Tübingen 1922, p.102.
11. See Troeltsch, 'Dies Krisis des Historismus', *Neue Rundschau* XXXIII, 1922, p.589.
12. Troeltsch, *Gesammelte Schriften*, Vol.3, p.67.
13. R. G. Collingwood, *The Idea of History*, Oxford University Press 1946, p.209.
14. F. Meinecke, *Die Entstehung des Historismus*, Munich and Berlin 1936, Vol.1, p.1.
15. Troeltsch, *Gesammelte Schriften*, Vol.4, p.338.
16. Troeltsch, *Protestantism and Progress*, Williams and Norgate 1912, p.34.
17. Cf. Troeltsch, *Gesammelte Schriften*, Vol.4, pp.573f.
18. In H. A. Hodges, *Wilhelm Dilthey: An Introduction*, Kegan Paul, Trench, Trubner, 1944, p.111.
19. Troeltsch, *Gesammelte Schriften*, Vol.3, p.24.
20. In *The Romantic Movement*, ed. A. Thorlby, Longmans 1966, p.84.
21. Troeltsch, *Gesammelte Schriften*, Vol.3, pp.66f.
22. Troeltsch, in *Encyclopedia of Religion and Ethics*, ed. J. Hastings, Vol.6, p.720.
23. Troeltsch, *Gesammelte Schriften*, Vol.3, p.55.
24. Troeltsch, op. cit., pp.675-9, cf. also p.28, n.14.
25. Troeltsch, op. cit., p.156.
26. K. Bornhausen, 'Ernst Troeltsch und das Problem der wissenschaftlichen Theologie', *Zeitschrift für Theologie und Kirche* IV, 1923, pp.196-223.

27. Troeltsch, 'Geschichte und Metaphysik', *Zeitschrift für Theologie und Kirche* VIII, 1898, p.69.

28. Tübingen, Freiburg i. B., and Leipzig 1900.

29. Troeltsch, *Zeitschrift für Theologie und Kirche* VIII, 1898, p.68.

30. Troeltsch, op. cit., p.6.

31. Troeltsch, *Gesammelte Schriften*, Vol.3, p.33.

32. Troeltsch, *Gesammelte Schriften*, Vol.2, pp.729-53.

33. Troeltsch, op. cit., p.732.

34. Troeltsch, op. cit., p.734.

35. Troeltsch, op. cit., p.738.

36. Troeltsch, 'The Dogmatics of the "religionsgeschichtliche Schule"', *American Journal of Theology* XVII, 1913, p.10.

37. *Die Absolutheit des Christentums und die Religionsgeschichte*, Tübingen ²1912; ET *The Absoluteness of Christianity*, SCM Press 1971.

38. See A. C. Bouquet, *Is Christianity the Final Religion?*, Macmillan 1921, p.205.

39. *American Journal of Theology* XVII, 1913, p.9.

40. *Christian Thought: Its History and Application*, University of London Press 1923.

41. *American Journal of Theology* XVII, 1913, p.11.

42. Troeltsch, *Gesammelte Schriften*, Vol.2, p.397.

43. Troeltsch, op. cit., p.511.

44. Troeltsch, op. cit., p.429.

45. *American Journal of Theology* XVII, 1913, p.13.

46. Troeltsch, *Gesammelte Schriften*, Vol.3, p.9.

47. E. Vermeil, *La pensée religieuse de Troeltsch*, Strasburg and Paris 1922, p.4.

48. Troeltsch, *Zeitschrift für Theologie und Kirche* VIII, 1898, p.9.

49. K. Stendahl, 'St Paul and the Introspective Conscience of the West', *Harvard Theological Review* LVI, 1963, pp.119-215.

50. H-G. Drescher, 'Das Problem der Geschichte bei Ernst Troeltsch', *Zeitschift für Theologie und Kirche* LVII, 1960, pp.186f.

III

THE EXISTENTIALIST RESPONSE

I T I S often suggested that the period of Western European history to which Troeltsch belonged was, until the outbreak of the First World War, one of relaxed and buoyant self-confidence in intellectual and social life. In the theological liberalism of which Troeltsch was, for many, the acknowledged leader, there obtained (it is said) a self-assurance, an exaltation of human achievement and an over-bold accommodation to the spirit of the age. The bubble of complacency was pricked, so the argument runs, only by the crisis of the war and its catastrophic aftermath in the Weimar Republic. But this was not Troeltsch's reading of the age in which he lived. Throughout his energetic intellectual career, he was deeply conscious of a widespread sense of powerlessness and anarchy pervading all spheres of life. The rise of industrialism, the growth of nationalism, the accelerating success of the physical sciences, the spread of popular Darwinism, the positivistic tendencies in the human sciences – these and other factors combined to cause a loss of bearings and a failure in confidence for his society. There was all too little sign of what Troeltsch called the 'mastery of the situation'. His own intellectual enterprise was directed towards precisely such a mastery; but he was very conscious of the difficulties which confronted him.

Throughout this period, according to Troeltsch, churchly

theology struggled to safeguard the power and autonomy of its traditional assertions. This theology could be likened to a retreating army, regularly obliged to take up new and hastily dug positions in the face of an advancing enemy. It was repeatedly forced back upon an ever narrower front, had to suffer heavy casualties and ran the risk of outright defeat. For theology's problems were not simply of its own making, were not simply movements and counter-movements in a private history. They were also, and for the greater part, the product of a massive change in thought and feeling brought about by historicism. It was not a question of a little local crisis, of liberalism as a fashionable reaction to fashionable trends, but of nothing less than the formidable consequences ensuing from what Troeltsch called the 'genesis of the modern world'. Historicism represented an irreversible tendency of the greatest moment, affecting life and thought in all respects. We have seen that, for Troeltsch, it was now impossible to imagine that fixed and absolute points could be identified by which we might judge and explain the processes of historical life. Not least was he critical of those theological tendencies which claimed to preserve such points of reference, thereby in turn claiming an immunity from those historical ways of thought which must govern all the human sciences. It is therefore important to appreciate, in relation to the theological movement which I shall discuss in this chapter, that Troeltsch did not regard his own undertakings as a sudden response to a sudden crisis. It was the repeated recrudescence of churchly theology during the nineteenth and early twentieth centuries which constituted such a response, bearing all the marks of crisis-religion, all the aspects of an emotional and unmeasured reaction to a situation superficially diagnosed.

Following Troeltsch, theology has viewed the situation very differently. There has been a widespread desire to challenge Troeltsch's axiom that theology may not stand apart from the inroads of historical science. There has been a tendency to treat Troeltsch's own position as a dominant but short-lived movement after which theology will wisely and properly return to its traditional ways. On this view Troeltsch is principally an aberration. From 1920, and for some forty years, a deal of the theology undertaken in Europe and North America was dominated by the thesis that the problem of history could appropriately be met by confining theological science to an area where historical science did not, and could not, operate. I propose to call this the 'existentialist response'. This may seem too imprecise a term to cover a wide range of theological writers. But it captures a common characteristic, namely that 'existence' rather than 'history' is the proper subject-matter of theology. In many respects, this response is no more than a fresh presentation of the position which Troeltsch so vigorously assailed. But in some of these subsequent writers the tradition which Troeltsch rejected is modified at certain important points. Furthermore, some significant concessions are made to Troeltsch's own standpoint. We must therefore ask whether this response represents a legitimate theological position in a world-view marked by historicism, or whether it is a false response, seeking to undo the work of a revolution in thought which cannot be undone.

I shall, for the most part, deal only with Rudolf Bultmann. Though he is regarded by some as an eclectic theologian in view of his supposed dependence upon Heidegger, I am clear that he is effectively representative of the existentialist response and that its main theses are present in his work. Bultmann's writings have of course attracted a large volume of expository and critical interest, so that his general position is widely known. In this chapter I intend to investigate his point of view relating to the problem of history and to set it in contrast with that of Troeltsch. It will also remain to be asked how Bultmann's scheme of thought can meet the challenge thrown down by the death of the past and the pull of the future. In the first place, however, I shall comment on how the group of theologians which included Bultmann viewed Troeltsch and the liberal movement with which he is normally associated.

For those theologians (including Barth, Bultmann and Gogarten) who were contributing in the 1920s to the new periodical *Zwischen den Zeiten*, Ernst Troeltsch symbolized the end of an age and the breakdown of a tradition. Brunner expressed this trenchantly as follows: 'To Ernst Troeltsch, who may perhaps be called the greatest and most modern of modernists, belongs the credit of having discerned and shown the irreconcilable contradiction which modern theology has so long attempted to hide. He saw and confessed, boldly and without equivocation, the chasm which separates modern theology from the theology of the Reformers and of the Ancient Church. But Troeltsch ... introduces also the final stage of this development. From AD 1700 to AD 1900 Christian theology changes its distinctively Christian bearings and drifts with an idealistic immanence-faith into theological liberalism. The year 1900 marks the approximate date when it began to sink into a sea of relativistic scepticism.'[1] Again Barth may be quoted on Troeltsch and other similar theologians that they 'hardly knew what to do to take care of the profusion and variety of the facts of life. They felt they must be impartial at all costs to the whole of creation and to every creature; and they became so generously impartial, that Christianity, having no special privileges with them, found itself the unhappy victim of an housing shortage.'[2] Again: 'I listened to [Troeltsch] ... with the dark foreboding that it had become impossible to advance any farther in the dead-end street where we were strolling in relative comfort.'[3] And again Barth writes: 'It was obvious that with [Troeltsch] the doctrine of faith was on the point of dissolution into endless and useless talk, and that for all the high self-consciousness of its conduct Neo-Protestantism in general had been betrayed on to the rocks, or the quicksands.'[4] Again Brunner writes: 'Troeltsch, the outstanding leader of this whole theological school, has formulated its essential common confession of faith. It is admirable in the frankness with which it expresses the renunciation of all that is specifically Christian.'[5] Bultmann also observes: 'The error is not that men did this historical work and obtained results which are more or less radical; rather, it is that they did not understand the significance of such work nor the meaning of the enquiry.'[6] From quotations such as these we can see the existence of common ground among those who, in the 1920s, reacted so sharply against Troeltsch. What Troeltsch had regarded as the liberating and exciting opening-up of the historical world meant for those theologians nothing less than a betrayal of Christianity. What Troeltsch saw as the release of theology from a restrictive meta-history, those theologians treated as the insertion of specifically Christian faith into the endless relativities of cultural history. Above all, these theologians accused Troeltsch of confining God inextricably within the mesh of human achievement, whereas, for them, 'God represents the radical negation and sublimation of man'.[7] On these grounds the historicizing of theology had to be challenged, whatever may or may not be said in respect of the other human sciences. It was not, as Bultmann makes clear, that the liberal theologians had nothing significant to say. Instead it was in their principal tendency that they were utterly mistaken.

For Bultmann there was one crucial respect in which neo-orthodox theology marked, not the rejection, but the confirmation of liberal theology. The neo-orthodox could not but welcome the way in which liberal theology had dealt a death-blow to metaphysical theologies of history. Furthermore they had demonstrated only too clearly that amid the relativity of all historical life no firm and fixed criteria can be found from which secure ethical and religious attitudes can be developed. Again, the new historical method had

shown that all historical judgments yielded no more than
probability and could not serve as a basis for faith. Thus it
seems that Bultmann could echo most of Troeltsch's conclusions as to the consequences of historicism. But in fact he
distorts Troeltsch's position at important points. In fact the
version of historicism to which Bultmann subscribed was
precisely that secondary, wretched *Historismus* to whose
overcoming Troeltsch devoted most of his mature intellectual life. Bultmann seemed only too ready, for reasons
which will become clear, to treat history as a closed system
of casual connections, whereas Troeltsch, in his primary use
of *Historismus*, had been at great pains to show that cultural
history is governed by a principle of causality quite different
from that employed in the natural sciences. So for Bultmann, and for Barth to only a slightly lesser extent, the
history of man in general, and of religious man in particular,
belongs to wretched *Historismus* with its anarchy of values.
From history as Troeltsch understood it, there is no way in
to Christian belief and thus no starting-point for Christian
theology. In consequence Bultmann can applaud the historical enterprise on the grounds that, the further it goes
and the more success it achieves, so the more it confirms its
inadequacy as a basis for faith. Thus Barth can write:
'Historico-critical research represents the deserved and
necessary end of *the* "foundations" of this understanding
(of faith)'.[8] This means, on Bultmann's view, that the entire
and detailed operation of biblical and historical research is
conducted with one negative goal in view, namely to establish its irrelevance for the theological enterprise. Bultmann
contends that historical criticism is needed 'to train us for
freedom and veracity' and to bring us to 'the realization that
the world which faith wills to grasp is absolutely unattain-
able by means of scientific research'.[9] This represents a
strange comment on the fact that much of Bultmann's
scholarly life has been devoted to precisely such painstaking
historical research, though it becomes more credible when

we consider the sceptical conclusions at which Bultmann arrived with his study of the New Testament documents. For central to his whole position is the view that Christ, as he bears upon faith, is not known historically. 'Anyone who does not yet know ... that we *cannot* any longer know Christ after the flesh should let himself be taught by critico-biblical research that the more radically he is horrified, the better it is for him and for the cause.'[10] So the real significance of Bultmann's position cannot be appreciated until we perceive that, principally, he was concerned to defend and preserve the Lutheran understanding of *sola fide*. To be *pure* faith, faith must not be dependent upon any mediating history, mysticism or metaphysics. Any such support for faith would compromise its radical character. It is in this context that Bultmann's treatment of history is set. I propose to show forth the main features of this treatment by considering his response to Luther, Herrmann and Heidegger.

Writing about the beginnings of neo-orthodoxy, Pannenberg has observed that 'one can feel here a proximity to the Luther-research ... flourishing at the same time'.[11] The crucial and creative period of Bultmann's own career certainly coincided with a substantial renaissance in Luther studies among such scholars as Holl and Seeberg. To account for this revival of interest in Luther it may well be right to see a reaction against the influential 'lives of Jesus' so that theologians could again assert that revelation is a contemporary as well as a historical reality. Closely bound up with this appeal to Luther is the Kant research of the period. In 1904 Bruno Bauch had drawn a parallel between dogmatic and intrinsic belief in Luther and theoretical and practical reason in Kant.[12] Thus, for Bultmann, faith is able to apprehend that reality which is beyond the reach of theoretical understanding.

The first edition of Karl Holl's 'Collected Essays' (including his studies on Luther) was published in 1921; Bultmann's programmatic essay on 'Liberal Theology and the Latest

Theological Movement' appeared in 1924.[13] Holl reserved
special attention for Luther's hermeneutical method. He
observes that Luther's exegesis involves the attempt, e.g. in
the Psalms, to relate the text to Christ. He shows that for
Luther the literal sense of scripture reveals Christ, whereas
the tropological sense yields the gospel. If the literal sense
yields Christ's sufferings and glory, the tropological sense
discloses 'what these mean for a man, how he may appropriate these for himself, and how he can go on experiencing
them himself in his own person'. In this way God speaks
to a man through the agency of scriptures. Holl writes:
'At a specified moment God gives power to the Word, so
that it makes its appearance to a man in the form of a
word spoken at that present and directed personally to him.'
'The man who is struck by this word comes, through this
medium, into contact with God Himself; he experiences the
point which is intended in the Word, and from then on he
learns how to understand the Word.'[14]

On this view, the true understanding of scripture is
apparently not derived by means of a scientific or historical
approach to interpretation. *Foris audire* is contrasted with
intus audire. Holl remarks that in the case of *intus audire*
Luther continually emphasizes that emotion which is the
work of the Holy Spirit. 'For nobody can understand God
or God's word aright without the means of the Holy Spirit.'[15]
The fact *that* the Word seizes a man at a certain moment is
also the work of the Holy Spirit. '[*Evangelium*] *enim advehit
spiritum.*'[16] Holl's interpretation of Luther is accurately
reflected in a passage where Bultmann expresses his views
on the same subject: 'To deem something true is not the
same thing as faith. Luther realized this, when in his exposition of the second article of belief, he subordinated all dogmatic statements to the one proposition, "I believe that
Jesus Christ ... is my Lord." Or when, in his lecture on the
Epistle to the Romans, he says: "To believe in Christ means
to be directed to him with the whole heart, to orientate

everything in his direction." To believe in Christ does not mean deeming true lofty teaching about his person, but rather believing the word, in which he addresses us, and through which he wants to become our Lord.'[17] This in turn mirrors the interpretation of Luther which Seeberg offered in his book of 1929.[18] God's work must be communicated to man so that it is available for him and appropriable by him. The work of God is thus made real for us through the Word. Unless the Word (Seeberg writes) transforms the historical event into existential history, that event will remain inaccessible to us and unfruitful for us. This, as will be clear, is very close to Bultmann's own point of view.

It is important, however, to recognize an important difference between Bultmann and Luther. In his book on Bultmann, H. P. Owen has noted four ways in which the notion of God's 'Word' is employed in Christian tradition:[19] the Person of the Eternal Son; the creative Word, maker of the world; the incarnate Word; the spoken Word that God addresses to men. Owen contends that Bultmann has discarded all but the last of these. 'Luther's belief', on the other hand (as Bauch puts it), 'is in its content wholly the dogmatic creed of Christendom.'[20] Luther, unlike Bultmann, relates the *dogmatic* statements to the situation in which man finds himself. In the section of the short catechism which deals with the article of redemption Luther asks, 'What does this mean?' His answer runs: 'I believe that Jesus Christ, very God, born of the Father in eternity, and also very man, born of the Virgin Mary, is *my* Lord, who has redeemed *me*, a lost and damned man, and has won and delivered *me* from all sins, from death, and from the power of the devil ...'[21] This is Luther's *pro me*. So, following Diem's analysis, we find that Luther thinks personalistically in his anthropology and ontologically in his doctrine of God.[22] It is always tempting to separate these two aspects so that dogmatic statements are dissolved into existential

statements: but in Luther the two are inseparably connected. Iwand, in a most important article, has shown that
after Kant the *pro me* of Luther lost its dogmatic basis and
was elevated on its own account into a formal epistemological method by analogy with Kant's practical reason. So,
according to Iwand, from Ritschl and Herrmann to Bultmann and Gogarten the *pro me* is employed in such a
way that a gulf is set up between dogmatic, ontological,
historical statements and personalistic, existential statements.[23]

From this analysis of the connection between Bultmann
and contemporaneous Luther research we can conclude: (1)
that Bultmann broadly agrees with Luther in the inner
connection which he establishes between the Word, the
event and faith, but that (2) Bultmann, following Kant,
modifies Luther's treatment of the Word as a communica-
tion and realization of the event of salvation, by separating
this realization from its historical and dogmatic basis in
Christ's work. Here lie the origins of Bultmann's distinction
between *Historie* and *Geschichte*.

The significance of Wilhelm Herrmann as a decisive con-
tributor to Bultmann's theological development has not been
adequately acknowledged. It is of considerable importance
for understanding why, how, and to what extent, Bultmann
turned to Heidegger. The sequence of dependence is made
clear in a remark of Bultmann dating from 1955. 'Heidegger
became of such importance for me just because I saw here
how certain definite intentions of W. Herrmann's theology
were clarified.'[24] In *The Communion of the Christian with
God*[25] Herrmann's 'definite intentions' are clearly visible.

According to Herrmann, much Christian doctrine pur-
ports to be information about God vouchsafed by revelation.
But it is not in this area that we come face to face with the
reality which gives to faith its certainty. Instead, God makes
himself known to us through a fact by virtue of which we
are able to believe in him. This fact is nothing other than

the appearance of Jesus in history as the reality of God, of which an account has been preserved in the New Testament. This means that we encounter Jesus as an undoubted reality amid the reality to which we ourselves belong. Thus, in order to come to God, we do not have to turn our backs on the actual historical life and relationships in which we stand. For it is precisely out of life in history that God comes to meet us. But what is the relationship between God meeting us in our reality and the appearance of Jesus of Nazareth as recorded in the New Testament?

Herrmann is clear that, given the methods and results of historical-critical research, we cannot make faith dependent upon so uncertain a basis. 'Those who like us demand the full freedom of historical criticism, which raises problems about all historical facts, ought not to want to ground faith upon the doubtfulness of a historical fact.'[26] Again Herrmann writes: 'A Christ fetched out from behind the New Testament tradition cannot be the ground for faith.'[27] At the same time Herrmann insists that there is no entry to Christ as the object of faith without reference to scripture and the Christian tradition. So he seeks to establish the ground of faith in the Christian proclamation, or rather in the Christ who is proclaimed. 'What we feel as an incontestable reality, what every man finds present in the sense that it belongs to his own reality, is the Christian proclamation which has as its content the revelation of God in Christ.'[28] So the real, historic Christ on whom faith depends, is the preached Christ. But 'it is not correct to call the composite Christ-picture of the New Testament the historic Christ'.[29] Herrmann's intention is to envisage a historic Christ who is not dependent upon the vagaries of New Testament research and who is part of our reality. So he appeals to the 'inner life of Jesus'. This 'inner life' can be detached from the historical-biblical tradition. Indeed Herrmann goes so far as to say that a man can come upon this inner life quite apart from that tradition; it has (it seems) an independent existence. The 'inner life of Jesus' consists in Jesus' Messianic consciousness, the meaning of his Messianic work, and the consciousness that he would accomplish this work by his death. Thus, 'the person of Jesus becomes to us a real power rooted in history, not through historical proofs, but through the experience produced in us by the picture of his spiritual life which we can find for ourselves in the pages of the New Testament'.[30] This leads Herrmann to conclude that 'the only thing of importance is to elevate above everything else that present experience in which we and others feel that the power of Jesus really exercises an inward compulsion upon us and lifts us out of ourselves'.[31]

Along these lines, Herrmann contends that we can avoid the difficulties of basing our faith upon facts which may only be probabilities, relying instead upon the power of Jesus, his inner life, as understood and retained by men who witnessed it, and as preserved among subsequent men in whom it had its effect. So Herrmann can say that the basis of faith is unchanging whatever the results of historical-critical study. Historical criticism has therefore a real, but negative, value. It clarifies that we cannot expect a scientific historical method to define the meaning of Jesus for the Christian. Criticism destroys false props to faith and continually gives us fresh standards against which to test the truth of that inner life of Jesus. This recalls G. Krüger's understanding of the role of scientific theology as imperilling souls, leading into doubt and shattering naïve belief.[32] 'A person truly awakened to faith hears quite calmly that much stands in the Bible which never can and was never meant to become part of our own intellectual property; for example, the whole ancient theory of nature and the traces of rabbinical theology and Jewish eschatology in the New Testament. When a truly earnest faith sure of its ground freely acknowledges this ... it will give free scope to that historical enquiry about the Bible which is the scientific task of theology.'[33]

We can see from this account that Herrmann interprets 'faith' to mean a free act of decision, of trust, which is an act of the historical-personal life *(ein Akt des geschicht-lichen Lebens)*. This act becomes a possibility 'whenever a personal life touches us, to which we can belong in trust and respect'.[34] Herrmann is endeavouring to avoid all contact with what can only be historical uncertainties. Following the Baden school of neo-Kantianism, and Lotze, he is seeking to draw a distinction between on the one hand the material world which is to be interpreted mechanistically, and on the other hand, the personal reality of God and of human experience. For, in Herrmann's own words, 'religion is not like a natural science or ethics, a body of generally recognized and accessible material'.[35] Thus, on the concept of miracle, he writes that 'the supernatural is to be classed with the discoveries of spiritualism which (if they exist) can still arouse the astonishment of savages, but for the civilized man only signify an extension of the known world'.[36] On the positive side Herrmann has developed an understanding of history, of being-in-history *(Geschichte)*, which cannot apparently be undermined by any kind of critical, worldly understanding. This view of *Geschichte*, rooted in a doctrine of experience, has been well characterized by Mahlmann. It is a 'unitary, original reality ... that unity between world and self which is grounded in life and accomplished in experience'.[37] But equally this view entails our admitting, as Mahlmann acknowledges, that *Geschichte* cannot ever be visibly recognized. There is no scientific method, appropriate to *Geschichte*, by which we might establish objectively that *Geschichte* is other than an illusion.

Before we examine how Bultmann develops Herrmann's point of view, two critical observations are necessary. In the first place we must take note of Herrmann's naïveté in supposing that the inner life of Jesus is a given element which can be detached from the results of historical-critical research. It is in fact dependent on the picture of Jesus which emerges from a critical study of the documents. Since the whole question of Jesus' Messianic vocation and consciousness is very much a matter of debate, it cannot serve as the kind of basis which Herrmann proposes. In the second place, and because this is so, Herrmann does not in fact keep the decision of faith as the act of historical-personal life in the way that he claims. That faith is dependent upon our being able to see in the New Testament the faith of Jesus.

By way of summary, we can note in Herrmann five principal theses.

1. Only out of life in history can God come to meet us.

2. Jesus is an element of that historical reality in which we stand.

3. The power, the inner life, of that historical *(geschicht-lich)* Jesus is to be found amidst the present life of men.

4. The fact of this inner life is supposedly independent of the New Testament record.

5. The absence of historical certainty is not an embarrassment; on the contrary, it removes false props to faith. In these five theses we must observe that history *(Geschichte)* is located in the sphere of experience and trust. It is not a phenomenon which lends itself to any kind of scientific or objective study.

Bultmann pursues Herrmann's intentions, but modifies the account at one crucial point. Bultmann insists, as we have seen, that the inner life of Jesus cannot have an existence independent of our critical judgment of the historical documents. So Herrmann has departed from what Bultmann believes to be the authentic Lutheran position. For the proclamation is not a proclamation *about* the inner life and power of Jesus. Notwithstanding, Bultmann acknowledges his debt to Herrmann. He was 'struggling (even if he does so with an inadequate body of abstract categories) to comprehend human being as "being-in-history" '.[38] For Bultmann, however, it was precisely here that Heidegger became

of importance, for he *did* provide an adequate body of categories for this purpose. Where, at the critical point, Herrmann confused the distinction between historical and *geschichtlich* aspects of the Christian proclamation, Heidegger
provided a basic clarification which accords exactly with the
Lutheran understanding of *sola fide*. Heidegger takes as his
starting-point not the external connection of events, with
their different determining factors, which we normally call
history. Instead, history refers to the way in which the
subjective form of human existence is inwardly structured.
This becomes clear from Heidegger's procedure in *Sein und
Zeit*.[39] To show how personal being *(Dasein)* is constituted,
Heidegger explores the theme of temporality *(Zeitlichkeit)*.
It is in this context that he develops his understanding of
historically *(Geschichtlichkeit)*. He has already shown how
personal being faces forward, especially towards death. He
now considers how personal being stretches along between
birth and death. Heidegger will not allow that this connectedness of life is to be accounted for as the sum of
momentary human experiences in time. Instead, he wants
to insist that the connectedness of time lies within the very
being of *Dasein*. So the moment of existence is not defined
in terms of factors in our life and environment but in terms
of the way in which personal being stretches itself out. We
can therefore say that personal being is not temporal because it stands in history; but that it exists historically
because it is temporal in the very basis of its being. This
distinction allows Heidegger to postulate a primary and a
secondary sense of history as he postulates two corresponding meanings of time. There is world-time *(Weltzeit)* which,
as van der Meulen has suggested, is, as in the philosophy of
nature, space-time at the primary level; and temporality
(Zeitlichkeit) which is not itself 'in time' in the sense of
'natural time'.[40] When these distinctions are translated into
a theological framework, Bultmann is obliged to say that
it is towards personal being with its intrinsic temporality

that revelation must address itself. It follows that neither revelation nor salvation can be organically related to external history. As Heidegger says: 'We contend that what is *primarily* historical is *Dasein*.' 'That which is secondarily historical is what we encounter within-the-world.'[41] So, for Heidegger, *Historie* means the science of history, whose subject-matter is those entities other than *Dasein* which belong to the world. *Geschichte*, on the other hand, refers (as we have seen) to the inner structure of *Dasein* which is not in any way dependent upon what we encounter within the world. In Bollnow's definition, *Geschichte* is 'the subjective structural form of such beings which in their inner meaning are determined in such a way that they have a history'.[42]

Now it would be a mistake to set Troeltsch's and Heidegger's understandings of history in total opposition. We must observe, however, that where Bultmann, Herrmann and Heidegger create an historical dualism, Troeltsch maintains a unitary view of history. Troeltsch is not in total opposition to the other point of view, for, as we have seen, he develops a view of *Historismus* which sees the formation of history in the acts and self-consciousness of individual human beings and collectivities. This is the chief burden of his account of individuality and development, leading to an appropriate account of historical causality. At the same time Troeltsch asserts that such history is not confined to the inner life of individuals but is realized in concrete, historical life and movement. Furthermore, cultural history is a perpetual interplay between the initiatives of individuals and groups, and the external factors of nature, geography, climate – in fact all the elements of contingency which belong to embodied life on this planet. For Troeltsch, it is quite misleading to speak of an external and internal history. On Troeltsch's view history has a very exposed character since it is open to, and in part constituted by, the total environment in which man is set. Yet this history has its own inwardness, for it is also constituted by the deeds of men shaping the individual totalities of history, initiatives which (as we have seen in Troeltsch's metalogic) reflect the very nature and immanent activity of God in history.

I am clear, following Diem and Ott rather than Körner, that Bultmann does end up with an historical dualism.[43] Ott writes: 'History is consequently split up into two different spheres of being. By this split, the unity of history, the possibility of a unitary-universal conception of history taking in all historical reality ... is lost.'[44] Körner's attempt to argue that Bultmann is not speaking about two spheres of reality, but about two aspects of the same reality, is not convincing. If this were the case Bultmann would not need to say that the association of *Historie* and *Geschichte* in a certain event is paradoxical. If the *historisch* and *geschichtlich* elements were aspects of the same reality, then we should expect the *geschichtlich* aspect to 'show through' in the historical aspect – which is precisely Luther's position.

Where, in the light of our discussion in this lecture, are we to locate that precise point of difference between Troeltsch on the one hand, and Bultmann, Herrmann and Heidegger on the other hand, which issues in a unitary and a dualist understanding of history respectively? Clarity on this question is crucial to the theme of my whole argument, since I shall suggest that only a unitary understanding of history can furnish a theological method which is able to respond to the death of the past and the pull of the future. For the dualist understanding of history, confining meaning to inner and individual personal being, can only lead to a theology which has no basis for responding creatively to historical movements and possibilities on a supra-individual level and for entering fruitfully into a discussion of the social, economic, political and other questions which dictate the future of cultural history. Where then does the presupposition lie which governs Bultmann's thoroughly consistent analysis of history? It has been a common practice to say that in this regard Bultmann is indebted to Heidegger. Thus the question as to Bultmann's presupposition would become a question about Heidegger's presupposition. I am, however, convinced that such an approach is mistaken. The way in which I have handled the theme of this chapter has been intended to show that in fact Heidegger's existentialism is only of marginal influence for Bultmann. As Bultmann himself said, Heidegger's analysis only *clarified* certain theological motives and emphases which were already in his possession. I propose, therefore, that Bultmann is to be taken with complete seriousness when in 1954 he wrote, 'as a matter of fact I do not build any theology upon Heidegger's philosophy', and that Heidegger is likewise to be heeded when he wrote in the same year, 'Bultmann does not build any theology upon my philosophy'.[45] Indeed, although it is not a topic which requires any detailed investigation in the present context, I incline to the view that Heidegger was probably more indebted to Bultmann than Bultmann to Heidegger. We must recall that Bultmann's basic intentions were already well-developed before Heidegger came to Marburg in 1923 and that Heidegger was closely involved with Bultmann and von Soden in the co-editorship of *Theologische Rundschau* from 1926 to 1936. However this may be, I should judge Müller to be correct when he says that the major themes of *Sein und Zeit* reveal a treatment of the problems raised which would be unthinkable without reference to the themes and methods of German evangelical theology in the Luthern tradition – a tradition by no means uniformly faithful to the character of Luther's own theological impulses.[46]

In this chapter I have tried to show that Bultmann consistently seeks to safeguard a concept of radical faith, *sola fide*. What underlies this central and all-embracing concern? It depends upon nothing less than a thoroughly negative assessment of the human situation both for man himself and for man before God. Malevez has commented on *Sein und Zeit*, linking Heidegger and Bultmann in a manner which I judge to be accurate, in the following terms: 'The philosophy of *Sein und Zeit* (at least in the way in which Bultmann and many others understand it) accentuates, in the concept of *Dasein*, the features which emphasize man's fall and misery. On the other hand, in his thought Bultmann has already a preconceived idea of the Christian message, fairly typical of Protestant thought, which lays great emphasis upon the idea of the Fall: the *aversio a Deo*, which is man's sin, constitutes a radical fall, a fundamental corruption of nature, a total loss of the image of God.'[47] Exactly the same point, though arrived at by quite different means, is made by Ogden in *Christ without Myth*.[48] We recall that Bultmann makes only one exception to his rule that all talk of God must be demythologized – namely those statements which refer to God as 'acting'. These are not mythological but analogical statements. Ogden makes the penetrating observation that the retention by Bultmann of the notion of God's 'action' as non-mythological is only a necessity because Bultmann has, without mention, inconsistently retained a mythological understanding of human nature as fallen. If Bultmann were to admit that his understanding of fallen human nature was mythological he would be able to allow that talk of God 'acting' is mythological and could therefore be free to develop an understanding of divine initiative more appropriate to his general treatment of man's being-in-history. That Bultmann does not, and cannot, do this derives from a basic presupposition about the negativity of all human worldly life which controls at every point his theological approach to the problem of history. I should wish to contend that this impulse is common to all those theologians who make what I have called the existentialist response. In the light of the reasoning which I have put forward, it is hardly surprising that the experience of the First World War and of the early years of the Weimar Republic could be supposed to provide massive confirmation for the dialectical theologians of a theological premise which, they maintained, pointed to the negative and falsely Promethean character of all human history.

At first sight it may seem that the theological method which derives from Bultmann's position *is* in fact well-equipped to face boldly a death of the past and a pull of the future. For it apparently severs us thoroughly, and in an uncompromising way, from bondage to the past, and allows us to concentrate upon any present and any future. But this possibility is in fact more apparent than real. For a price has to be paid for this severance. A theology which can concentrate upon any present and any future is confined in its scope to the clarification and salvation of that individual *Dasein* which has no real connectedness with the empirical phenomena of cultural and natural history. It can as such have no bearing upon the problem which presents itself to human beings of choosing and realizing on a corporate scale one of a number of alternative futures. Nor, as was possible (at least in principle) for Troeltsch and Henson, does it provide any means, once a past for its own sake is experienced as dead, of relating the achievements and values of an historical past to the present and the future. The only yield of the past, on the existentialist view, is a set of understandings of personal *Dasein* which are separable from historical contexts as we normally understand them. Thus cultural history, against the unitary view which Troeltsch sets forth, becomes punctiliar in character. Koehler seizes on this punctiliar character of history in the following quotation: 'Dialectical theology has not yet submitted a history of the Church; its orientation in this field is, however, sufficiently clear. It consists of a repetition of the *historia sacra* in terms of an abrupt dualism between salvation history and human history.'[49] On this view, the possibility of historical growth, development and creative change (in Troeltsch's sense) cannot be accorded any theological justification. Indeed history must be interpreted *a priori* as if such historical growth, development and change were quite alien to theological understanding and *can there-fore only be* symptoms of a history of shipwreck of which the history of the Old Testament people is for Bultmann an example.

I judge, therefore, that Heinrich Ott is wholly mistaken in supposing that it is theoretically possible for Bultmann to enlarge his particular understanding of history to a point which would embrace world history.[50] I agree with Ott that Christian theology must seek to proceed in this direction, and in my last lecture I shall be concerned with the difficulties and possibilities which attend this task. But the movement towards a theological understanding of world-history cannot be advanced on the basis of a historical dualism deriving from an intuition about the thoroughgoing negativity of human, historical life. Can theology give full weight to that notion of God's initiative which the existentialists tried to safeguard, but without falling into their historical dualism? To respect the unitary view of history disclosed by historicism, is the theologian not obliged to question the thesis of the negativity of all human existence before God?

NOTES

1. E. Brunner, *The Theology of Crisis*, Scribner, New York 1929, p.7.
2. K. Barth, *The Word of God and The Word of Man*, Hodder and Stoughton 1928, p.148.
3. K. Barth, *Theology and Church*, SCM Press 1962, pp.6of.
4. K. Barth, *Church Dogmatics*, IV, 1, T. and T. Clark 1956, p.387.
5. E. Brunner, *The Mediator*, Lutterworth 1934, pp.68f.
6. R. Bultmann, *Faith and Understanding*, SCM Press 1969, p.30.
7. R. Bultmann, op. cit., p.29.
8. Quoted in Bultmann, op. cit., p.31.
9. Ibid.
10. Ibid.
11. W. Pannenberg, article 'Dialektische Theologie', *Die Religion in Geschichte und Gegenwart*, [3]1959, p.168.

12. B. Bauch, *Luther und Kant*, Berlin 1904, esp. p.34.

13. K. Holl, *Gesammelte Aufsätze zur Kirchengeschichte*, Tübingen ⁴1927, Vol.1, pp.544-82. Bultmann's essay is reprinted in *Faith and Understanding*, pp.28-52.

14. Holl, op. cit., p.548.

15. Luther, *Werke*, Weimar 1883ff., VII, 546, 24f.

16. Luther, op. cit., VIII, 459, 39.

17. R. Bultmann, *Glauben und Verstehen*, Vol.3, Tübingen 1960, p.126.

18. E. Seeberg, *Luthers Theologie, Motive und Ideen*, I. *Die Gottesanschauung*, Göttingen 1929.

19. H. P. Owen, *Revelation and Existence*, University of Wales Press 1957, p.57.

20. B. Bauch, *Luther und Kant*, p.23.

21. *Luthers Katechismen*, ed. Bertheau, Hamburg 1896, p.11.

22. H. Diem, *Dogmatics*, Oliver and Boyd 1959, pp.35ff.

23. H. Iwand, 'Wider den Missbrauch des "pro me" als methodisches Prinzip in der Theologie', *Theologische Literaturzeitung* LXXIX, 1954, cols.453-8.

24. From a letter quoted in G. W. Ittel, 'Der Einfluss der Philosophie M. Heideggers auf die Theologie Rudolf Bultmanns', *Kerygma und Dogma*, II, 1956, p.93.

25. Williams and Norgate ²1906, reprinted SCM Press 1972.

26. W. Herrmann, *Gesammelte Aufsätze*, Tübingen, 1923, p.184.

27. Herrmann, op. cit., p.315.

28. G. Niemeier, *Wirklichkeit und Wahrheit*, Gütersloh 1937, p.71.

29. Herrmann, *Gesammelte Aufsätze*, p.312.

30. Herrmann, *Systematic Theology*, Allen and Unwin 1927, p.51.

31. Herrmann, *The Communion of the Christian with God*, p.82.

32. G. Krüger, *Christliche Welt* XIV, 1900, pp.804-7.

33. Herrmann, *Faith and Morals*, Williams and Norgate 1910, pp.47ff.

34. Bultmann, *Glauben und Verstehen*, Vol.3, 1961, p.102.

35. Herrmann, *Gesammelte Aufsätze*, p.383.

36. Herrmann, op. cit., p.132.

37. T. Mahlmann, 'Das Axiom des Erlebnisses bei Wilhelm Herrmann', *Neue Zeitschrift für systematische Theologie* IV, 1962, p.82.

38. Bultmann, *Essays Philosophical and Theological*, SCM Press 1955, p.260.

39. M. Heidegger, *Being and Time*, SCM Press 1962.

40. J. van der Meulen, *Heidegger und Hegel*, Meisenheim/Glan ²1954, p.60.

41. Heidegger, *Being and Time*, pp.431, 433.

42. O. Bollnow, *Existenzphilosophie*, Stuttgart ³1949, p.102.

43. Diem, *Dogmatics*; H. Ott, *Geschichte und Heilsgeschichte in der Theologie Rudolf Bultmanns*, Tübingen 1955; J. Körner, *Eschatologie und Geschichte*, Hamburg 1957.

44. Ott, op. cit., p.17.

45. Quoted in Ittel, *Kerygma und Dogma* II, 1956, p.91.

46. G. Müller, 'Martin Heideggers Philosophie als Frage an die Theologie', *Theologische Zeitschrift* XV, 1959, p.363.

47. L. Malevez, *The Christian Message and Myth*, SCM Press 1958, p.37.

48. SCM Press 1962.

49. W. Koehler, article 'Kirchengeschichte I', *Die Religion in Geschichte und Gegenwart*, ³1959, p.895.

50. H. Ott, 'Rudolf Bultmann's Philosophy of History', in *The Theology of Rudolf Bultmann*, ed. C. Kegley, SCM Press 1966, p.63.

IV

THEOLOGY AND THE PHILOSOPHY OF HISTORY

WE MAY divide philosophy of history into two main genres. The first of these is represented by Hegel or, in more theological than philosophical strain, by Schlegel. Friedrich von Schlegel introduced his *Philosophy of History* in the following way : 'To point out historically in reference to the whole human race, and in the outward conduct and experience of life, the progress of [the restoration in man of the lost image of God] in the various periods of the world, constitutes the object of the "Philosophy of History".'[1] A more sober version is represented by Toynbee. In this genre we find an overarching interpretative principle *and* an appeal to historical evidence. The second genre is analytical or critical philosophy of history where, on the other hand, the chief task is to 'clarify and analyse the "idea" of history'.[2] This understanding of the philosophy of history has close affinities with philosophy of science and some links with that philosophy of religion which has been shaped by linguistic philosophy.

In this form, analytical philosophy of history is a recent phenomenon, emanating from the United States and the British Commonwealth since the Second World War.[3] There are, of course, obvious antecedents to such work. Troeltsch may in some respects be classified as an analytical philosopher of history. But the recent movement has for the most

part worked on a closely defined front, has been occupied
with a limited number of problems and has kept well clear
of speculative questions. It seems strange that theologians
have paid little attention to this analytical philosophy of
history when they have reacted vigorously to, and profited
from, contact with critical philosophy of religion as this
was given its characteristic impulse by a volume like *New
Essays in Philosophical Theology*.[4] There are, of course,
independent works such as T. A. Roberts' *History and Christian Apologetic*[5] and Van Harvey's *The Historian and the
Believer*.[6] But to no small extent the debate about theology
and history has followed lines laid down by the dominant
movements in recent German Protestant theology which
have been largely untouched by the kind of undertakings
associated with scholars such as Dray, Hempel, Mandelbaum
and Gardiner. It is not my intention in this lecture to offer
any detailed account of the way in which the concern of
analytical philosophers of history with historical explanation, historical causality and historical objectivity might be
related to specific instances of historico-theological interpretation of the biblical documents. Such enquiries certainly
deserve to be fostered. I want, however, to ask a more
general question about the relationship of this critical philosophy of history to the different procedures which the theologian might follow in seeking to elaborate a theological
understanding of the past, the present and the future. Can
there be found, directly or indirectly, any guidance for the
theologian in this task, whether in the form of warning or
encouragement? Before broaching this theme, however, I
propose to look broadly at the alternatives which are presented to the theologian, thus placing Troeltsch and Bultmann in a wider context than I have yet attempted. I take
the view that the structure of the problem concerning history and theology is very similar to the problem of the
relations of *theology and science*, and to the theological
problem of the relationship between *Christ, man and world*.

It is therefore worth asking whether these analogous themes can throw any light on our approach to the historical question.

The great medieval cosmologies were predominantly theological in character. In St Bonaventure, for example, the spheres are moved by God through a created power with his immediate co-operation. But then the medieval view underwent a revolution as momentous as the later revolution in history. The medieval picture of a perfect, static, hierarchical and anthropocentric world-order was shattered at the hands of Nicolas of Cusa, Marcellus Palingenius, Copernicus, Galileo Galilei and their successors. Since then, theology has never been able to live and work amid the harmonious unity of this world-view, where the cosmos seemed to vouch for the truth of the gospel and the gospel seemed to vouch for the truth of the cosmos. Once that delicately balanced unity was shattered, the theologian had to seek out new ways of understanding the relationship between a religious world-view and an aggressively independent scientific world-view. Despite the enormous diversity of theological responses to this problem, it is possible to isolate four general types of which many others are only variations.

1. The theologian may seek to evade the problem entirely by postulating a pan-religious interpretation of the cosmos. On this view, the cosmos is entirely transparent to the divine life. So, for Boehme, 'the universe is a single divine life; it is God's revelation in all things'.[7] This kind of approach recurs in Hegel, Schelling and Tillich. It is presented in a very attractive form in Friedrich Christoph Oetinger, who was a naturalist, a chemist and a doctor – as well as being a parson. Oetinger seeks to develop a *philosophia sacra* which unites God and nature, spirit and matter, and which sees Christ's appearance as the starting-point of a process which brings about the world's transformation.[8] With strong mystical and 'theosophical' influences, Oetinger is able to present a very consistent theological outlook. Re-

calling Teilhard de Chardin he was able, for example, to view his multifarious scientific interests as truly part of his worship of God. But there are formidable difficulties in this point of view. The world tends to lose its own ontological character; it is – to use the German word – *verweltlicht*. So too God is so closely identified with the immanent world-process that his independent, transcendent character is threatened; he is *vergöttlicht*. These are the prices which have to be paid for the unified view which the pan-religious scheme achieves. The other views which I shall mention all affirm the autonomy of the world and of the scientific world-view, whilst treating variously its implications for theology.

2. With the growing dualism between science and theology, God and world, spirit and nature, and with the reinforcement which Kant's philosophy was supposed to give to such a dualism, many theologians have avoided the risk that their own position might gradually be eroded by science. Instead, they have handed over to the scientist the entire responsibility for the interpretation of the natural order, whilst maintaining a separate supernatural world as the sole preserve of the theologian. On this view, the theologian has to say that certain doctrinal assertions which appear to refer to the empirical world are not in fact what they seem and must rather be given a 'purely theological' interpretation. So Emil Brunner writes: 'The Christian statement on Creation is not a theory of the way in which the world came into being – whether once for all, or in continuous evolution – but it is an "existential" statement.'[9]

3. The theologian, granting the autonomy of the physical world, may hope that the development of science will produce theories which will confirm and support certain doctrinal points of view. So it has been supposed that, somehow or other, biological theories of evolution would confirm the idea of a teleological process from divine creation to eschaton. Likewise, Heisenberg's indeterminacy principle was seized upon to provide (it was supposed) support for

theological claims about human and divine freedom.[10] On the whole, however, theologians have become more sensitive to the dangers of eliding different areas of thought, helped no doubt by the careful work which has been undertaken on the nature of religious language. But the theologian who properly takes fright at crude category mistakes may feel tempted to flee to the extreme position set out under 2. above.

4. The theologian may subscribe to the idea that there is an unchanging gospel and changing world-views. As a new world-view comes into currency, the theologian's task is to restate the gospel in the framework of that world-view in order to render the gospel more intelligible. This argument appears to safeguard theology's special interests. On the other hand, it presupposes that the theologian can in fact point unerringly to the unchanging gospel so that he can restate it. This in turn means that at one point or another, say in the New Testament writings, the theologian can separate the unchanging gospel from the world-view or world-views in which it is there framed. In fact there appears to be little consensus among theologians as to what constitutes the unchanging gospel. Moreover, this argument leaves the theologian without guidance as to how he shall proceed at any one time in respect of restatement when he is faced by competing and very different world-views.

As we look back over a long period of theological history since the shattering of the medieval world-view, it seems that none of these four alternative procedures are particularly satisfying. The pan-religious view appears to ride roughshod over the stubborn contingencies of the world. The dualist view has to renounce all interpretative claims over a major part of the reality in which we are set, thereby leaving the field wide open to all manner of other interpretations which may go far beyond scientific theories as such. The view which seeks confirmation of theological claims by an appeal to apparently congenial scientific theories often runs close to grave intellectual confusion. Moreover, the history of theology is full of the obituaries of such precarious correlations. The restatement theory founders not least because it supposes that a world-view is somehow a neutral framework of ideas. It seems then that the theologian must come to terms with the fact that there can be no settled relationship between theology and science. Rather we must think in terms of an exceptionally complex dialectical relationship in which, by definition, there are no absolutely fixed points. This is not of course to deny that the theologian may offer some illumination to those who elaborate a scientific world-view. Equally the theologian should expect to find from science some illumination in respect of his own characteristic concerns. But the theologian must at one and the same time be modest and courageous about his convictions. This means that all theological judgments have a provisional character whereby they are kept open to a concern for the truth of the gospel and alert to the dangers which come from an uncritical response to persuasive, not necessarily misleading, but always ephemeral scientific opinions.

At the beginning of this chapter I referred to the theological problem of Christ and world, as also presenting an instructive parallel with the historical question. Rainer Mayer in *Christuswirklichkeit*,[11] a remarkable study of Bonhoeffer's theological development, has shown how Bonhoeffer himself took up during his life several different standpoints to this question in sharp reaction to the attitudes adopted by his contemporaries. Meyer observes that the industrial-technological revolution with its accompanying break-up of social life had, since the nineteenth century, forced upon the church the need for a fresh interpretation of worldly reality. In this new situation, the church's first reaction was to despise and reject the new culture. Faith treated the world as wholly alien to itself and withdrew into 'Hinterweltlertum'. The second reaction of the church was to withdraw from his isolation and to seek a somewhat more positive understanding of the world. So there emerged what Mayer calls a 'pseudo-Lutheran doctrine of the two kingdoms', a this-worldly division between the sphere of the church and the sphere of the world. In this division, the sphere of the church was confined to the inner life of the consciously religious individual; all the rest was given over to 'world'. Mayer also notes a third, more recent proposal from the tradition of Protestant theology, namely a thoroughly positive evaluation of the world on the grounds that the autonomy of worldly life comes about as the necessary consequences of Christian faith. This third reaction, like the first, leads to withdrawal, but on different grounds. Concerning these three forms of reaction, Mayer observes: 'It is obvious that these three attempts at a solution of the problem, each of which is characteristic of a certain period in recent theological history, are still motivated by a simultaneous fear of, and fascination for, the industrial-technological revolution. Even the affirmation that the social break-up is the consequence of faith cannot conceal this anxiety, Faith is withdrawn from reality and is thus relieved of having to face any challenge from the autonomous world.'[12] It is not difficult to see that Bultmann is to be located amid this way of thinking.

Bonhoeffer's contribution to this question reveals yet another possible procedure for the theologian. 'He found a wholly new and bold solution. The world does not call Christ and his rule into question; rather Christ calls the world into question. The aim here is not to set up a new antithesis between Christ and world, but rather to overcome the existing antithesis. So Christ has entered the world. He has transformed and renewed its structures. Only in him does the world discover its authentic structure.' [13] This coming of Christ for such a purpose is visible in the church, but actually extends to the whole of worldly reality. Mayer concludes, however, that Bonhoeffer's system collapses because he does not allow the world to have its own proper ontology. Critical of a false dualism, Bonhoeffer leans over towards monism. But the world of empirical reality continually challenges this christological monism. Bonhoeffer, by taking up worldly reality into Christic reality, wrongly anticipates the consummmation which belongs to the eschaton. Mayer takes the view that in the *Letters and Papers from Prison* this artificial unity falls apart, leaving Bonhoeffer to find another way forward. But despite the collapse of the system, Bonhoeffer's basic theological premise can and must be maintained, namely the belief in the reality of Christ as a reality ontologically independent of the world and prior to it.

Mayer's penetrating analysis of Bonhoeffer's theological attitudes is exceptionally relevant to the historical question. In the light of that analysis and in the light of my consideration of the 'science and religion' debate, I now turn to examine directly some of the options which the theologian can take up his dealings with history. I shall mention four such options, drawing attention to the close parallel which the theologian faces with regard to science.

1. After the manner of Schlegel, he can seek to trace out an evident process of divine redemption amid the movements and experiences of worldly history. On this view we may say that history conforms to a divine plan or that history *is* that divine plan.

2. The theologian can adopt a theological premise which, it will be said, enables us comprehensively to review and refashion our understanding of history itself. Thus Moltmann claims in his *Theology of Hope* that, by virtue of the resurrection of Christ, there comes into being a new kind of history to which the old methods and criteria are no longer applicable.

3. The theologian can seek confirmation of his own theological approach in a congenial historical theory (if it is in fact a *historical* theory). An example of this procedure is

found in the use of Collingwood by Bultmann, James M. Robinson and Norman Sykes.[14]

4. The theologian can, in one way or another, dismiss history from the subject-matter of his theological enterprise in the manner of Bultmann, Gogarten and others. A similar motive is apparent in those theological undertakings in which history is withdrawn as the context of theological dogmas, leaving the dogmas with an independent, a-historical existence.[15]

If the theologian eschews any or all of these options, he seems condemned to speak, *qua* theologian, with a faint and halting voice. On the other hand the difficulties of each of these options are formidable.

1. The theologian who follows Schlegel or who adopts a pan-religious understanding of reality or a scheme of salvation history is not required to pay heed to any historical theory. His criteria of selection and description possess a purely theological character. This approach must run counter to the canons of historicism since it undermines human causality and autonomy, natural causality, and absolutizes one historical locus of redemption as the theological key to unlock all history. Recalling Bonhoeffer's position, it deprives the historical world of its own ontology. It is a defect which will be found in all idealist theories of history.

2. The notion of a new kind of history, caused by what is claimed to be (in part at least) a historical event, meets the difficulty that the same event which is supposed to create this history itself open to the challenge of historical criticism.

3. The theologian's attachment to a congenial theory of history tends to lose something of its force if the historical theory receives only limited support among philosophers of history and if it is in any case only one among many competing theories. (In fact there is some doubt whether the writers whom I mentioned earlier are faithful to Collingwood's own intentions.)

4. The thoroughgoing rejection of history, as irrelevant

and even dangerous to the theological enterprise, makes it impossible to advance theological interpretation beyond the sphere of the individual's inner life.

If these rebuttals are at all representative of the objections which can be raised against the procedures which I earlier outlined, then there are indications of an impasse. Are we obliged to say, as in the case of science, that we are left with a puzzling and complex dialectical relationship between theology and history which seems to rule out of court the establishment of fixed positions? Although I believe this to be a more accurate account of the true state of affairs than any of the other possibilities which I have so far considered, the matter cannot be left there. Such a statement of the position really gives no effective guidance to the theologian. Nor does it really take account of the definite constraints which *Historismus* imposes on the theologian. I shall consider these issues further by examining some of the implications of Bultmann's and Troeltsch's positions which did not come within the scope of chapters II and III.

In chapter I, I showed how Henson made the theologian's exegesis of history dependent upon the historian's ability to certify as reliable certain historical claims made in the documents of the New Testament. In chapter II, I showed that Troeltsch took much further than Henson this subordination of theology to history. Not only did Troeltsch recognize the difficulties which the theologian must encounter because historical judgments are always of probabilities and never of certainties, he also insisted that theological claims cannot in any case be made in reference to isolated events. Indeed, with the concepts of individuality and development, Troeltsch elaborated a historical logic which saw history as a network of reciprocal occurrence in which single events could not be open to special divine intervention. Even on the immanent level, Troeltsch saw further difficulties for the theologian. Historicism reveals an extraordinary diversity of theological ideas and movements. These defy capture under any single formula, any universally-valid 'essence of Christianity'. Thus, Troeltsch was left with a view of the theologian's task as consisting in the description and evaluation of past cultural-religious totalities which are brought into the present in the execution of the cultural synthesis. According to Troeltsch this theological purpose was faithful to the character of historical reality as disclosed by historical logic, and faithful also to the theological metalogic which the historical logic tentatively indicated.

Bultmann, on the other hand, clearly felt that Troeltsch's procedure meant the virtual dissolution of the central themes of Christian theology. He therefore (as he thought) took Troeltsch's argument to its obvious conclusion in giving over history to the historians and in relinquishing theological interest in all but that individual, inner history where the themes of revelation and faith could be expounded in a full and radical way, immune from the threats of critical history. We have already seen that, as a result of this project, Bultmann cannot develop a theology of history which goes beyond the privatized world of the individual. Where Troeltsch retained his grasp on the possibility of a material philosophy of history at the apparent expense of theological incisiveness, Bultmann maintained that incisiveness at the price of a historical dualism which consigns the principal part of human history to shipwreck and secularity. It seems as if neither Bultmann's nor Troeltsch's conclusions leave much room for manoeuvre to the theologian who would concern himself with history, as distinct from the existentialist exegete or the historian of religious culture. It deserves mention, however, that both scholars were reacting sharply to movements of thought which they regarded as a threat to the theologian's characteristic responsibility. That they might not have agreed about the nature of the theologian's responsibility is certainly true. But both Troeltsch and Bultmann reacted to a common enemy and in a way by no means uncharacteristic of many of their contemporaries. Thus, before being forced to accept or reject their proposals outright, it is wise to consider their interpretation of the threatening context in which they framed these proposals. For it may be that adjustments to their theories, on the ground that today the context has changed, may leave us with the possibility of adapting their theories in a manner which is fruitful for the present. I hold that this is in fact possible in the case of Troeltsch but not in the case of Bultmann.

As we have already seen, Troeltsch reacted vigorously to what he regarded as the improper intrusion of positivizing tendencies into the human sciences. He believed that a deterministic reading of the human sciences had grave consequences for political, social, intellectual and religious life. Thus, following his mentor Wilhelm Dilthey, Troeltsch argued that history differed from the natural sciences in respect of subject-matter, method and of the historian's intention. Here we are reminded of Windelband's essay on 'History and Natural Science' in his volume *Präludien*. 'The empirical sciences seek in the knowledge of the real either the general in the form of a law of nature or the particular in the historically determined structure. They observe in the one case the law that remains the same; in the other cases they observe the unique, self-defined content of the actual occurrence. One group is the law-sciences; the other is the occurrence-sciences.'[16] Although Troeltsch was critical of Windelband and Rickert for what he believed was their excessive imposition of *a priori* logical categories upon history, he shared (with Dilthey) their general intention to arrive at a historical method independent of the methods of natural science. In this motive, Troeltsch was deeply concerned to preserve the autonomy and reality of the religious element. To this extent Troeltsch stands in the tradition of Kant and his followers. Troeltsch's entire theological scheme was deeply imbued with Kant's moral vision.

But he departs from Kant, from Windelband and Rickert, and from the neo-Kantian tradition, in the importance which he ascribes to historical reality and to historical understanding. If history is a second world alongside that of natural science, it is within history that the ethical self exists; the ego is part of historical reality and fully determined by it. Against this, the *a priori* concepts of Kantianism appeared abstract and wholly logical in character. But once Troeltsch had recognized the historical conditionedness of all creations of the human spirit, once he had arrived at the notion of history as a complex interrelatedness of becoming, he naturally found it impossible to defend the absolute character of religious or ethical faith. So it appears that, in his concern to free the ethical and religious motive from dissolution in the causality of natural science, by postulating the independent character of historical reality, Troeltsch found himself with what looked like another parallel, virtually closed system of cultural history in which the search for transcendent value was difficult if not impossible. Admittedly, this view of historical reality salvaged the spontaneity and freedom of human history, but at the cost of a dangerously threatening 'anarchy of convictions' in the religious and ethical sphere. That Troeltsch did not intend or want this conclusion is evidenced in his religious metaphysics. He struggles there to conceive of the historical world as in some sense open to divine influence in a way that the world of nature is not.

Now Bultmann's position is in principle not very different from Troeltsch's. He too saw the danger of religious and ethical faith suffering rationalization in the scientific worldview. He accepted, with the same apparently uncritical ease as Troeltsch, that natural science is a closed system with its own tight, impenetrable causality. So Bultmann sets up a clear, iron-curtain distinction between what belongs to being-as-object and what belongs to being-as-self. This recalls Karl Jaspers' strict line of demarcation between the respective subject-matters of philosophical world-orientation and illumination of existence. But because *Historismus,* with its anarchy of convictions, appears to confirm his radical view of faith, Bultmann treats the place of history quite differently from Troeltsch. He divides *history* into being-as-object and being-as-self. Thus history-as-object, as well as science, is included in the category of 'world', i.e. as the antithesis to faith and revelation. It is clear that Bultmann is ultimately much closer than Troeltsch to the Kantian position. But we can observe that in both Troeltsch and Bultmann there is little interaction between the spheres which they have so carefully demarcated – in Troeltsch between scientific, historical and religious reality; in Bultmann between science and *Historie* on the other hand, and *Geschichte* and faith on the other hand. If, however, we can allow that there are in fact grounds for recognizing more interactive movement in these systems, then Troeltsch's becomes the infinitely more fruitful. For, in conformity with the revolution of historicism, he has given full and appropriate weight to the way in which history shapes and determines man's being in the world. Man is in, and part of, a world-history indeed. But that history cannot wholly be interpreted out of itself. The interpretation must be shaped by a multiplicity of factors which include scientific and religious understanding. With this crucial adjustment, Troeltsch's positive understanding of *Historismus* provides the essential context for the theologian's task.

To conclude this chapter I want to ask how the general position which I have now reached relates to the yield of analytical philosophy of history. I have already indicated that this critical theory of history has been heavily preoccupied with the questions of historical explanation, objectivity and causality. Perhaps the most dominant issue has concerned the extent to which historical explanation should be regarded simply as an instance of that kind of explanation which belongs to the sciences in general or how far it should be accorded a special status. This debate is often labelled as one between positivists (e.g. Hempel) and idealists (e.g. Collingwood). Thus Hempel can assert that historical explanation 'aims at showing that the event in question was not a "matter of chance", but was to be expected in view of certain antecedent or simultaneous conditions. The expectation referred to is not prophecy or divination, but rational scientific anticipation which rests on the assumption of rational laws.'[17] Against this, Collingwood writes: 'The disappearance of historical materialism, however, entails the further conclusion that the activity by which man builds his own constantly changing world is a free activity. There are no forces other than this activity which control it or modify it or compel it to behave in this way or in that, to build one kind of world rather than another.'[18] Now it can be argued that the weakness of the idealist position lies in the fact that it only takes into account the actions of human beings, and that a full acknowledgment of non-human factors would take us closer to Hempel's position whether in its original or modified forms. It seems more probable, however, that we should account for the differences between the two standpoints by asking about the historian's intention. It appears, on this criterion, that the positivist is primarily concerned to ask 'what made this event happen', whereas the non-positivist may be more concerned with questions of intelligibility or interpretation. The possibility of interpretation may depend upon our ability to relate together a multiplicity of occurrences under some organizing concept, under what Beard called an 'overarching hypothesis', which is quite different from a rational law.

In fact this distinction between positivist and idealist, however much the positions may have been refined since Popper and Hempel first stated the positivist case, is not a very helpful one. When we consider what historians do when they write history, we observe not one but many intentions. Exactly the same subject-matter may be treated

by the same historian with more than one canon of explanation in mind. The restriction of historical understanding,
as of historical causality, to one type seems also to run
counter to what may be called a commonsensical view of
history, namely that it is the complex product of a multiplicity of factors, natural and human, individual and collective, conscious and unconscious, chance and intention, and
so on. I agree therefore with Patrick Gardiner that 'the
conflict supposed to exist between materialistic and idealistic
interpretations of history is an illusory one. We are not
confronted by two realms of causes intersecting or running
across one another. What we are confronted by are various
uses of the word "explain".'[18] These different uses are
legitimate in view of the variety of historical material which
calls for explanation. They only really enter into com-
petition where they are extrapolated as world-views, when
we hypostasize different ways of talking about human beings
and their history, thereby failing to appreciate that these
different ways of talking about human beings are primarily
dictated by different interests on the part of the historian
in the face of infinitely detailed subject-matter.

If this is the case, then it seems that analytical philosophy
of history is not particularly productive in respect of guidelines for the theologian who is concerned with history. But
we may importantly conclude, looking very broadly at what
has been undertaken in this critical philosophy of history,
that a naïve theological interpretation of history is unlikely
to be faithful to the usual complexity of historical material.
To make this point in a more theological way, talk of God's
action or presence in history has to be so formulated that
it takes account, in its very structure, of the multifactoral
constitution of history. At the same time we have to
expect that this talk of God's action and presence will relate
to themes of sufficient concreteness for the historian to
grasp.

Finally, it seems clear that, on grounds of historical logic alone, there is no obvious connection between a certain theory of historical understanding and a certain view of the nature of historical reality. The historian is always involved in a process of selection which is dictated both by his own interests and by the nature and availability of the subject-matter. The grounds on which the historian engages in the selection that he does are many and complex. When, for example, we talk about causation in history, we single out one or several conditions as more relevant than others in a way which in part depends on our personal moral attitudes. The primary difficulty which the theologian meets is not that his presuppositions necessarily come into conflict with the nature of historical reality. Troeltsch was too dogmatic on this score because he made too swift a transition from historical logic to historical world-view. The theologian's problem turns more upon his ability to interpret history in an intelligible way. William Dray, in his critique of Niebuhr, has shown how easy it is for the theologian to present a theology of history which does not actually say anything about history.[19] Somehow or other the theologian must speak in concrete terms and he must respect the ontology of worldly reality. But if he abides by these conditions, can the theologian speak of God's presence or action in history in a way which at all makes clear that it is God and not simply man who is active and present in history? If this can be done at all, I take the view that it will not be achieved simply on the basis of a conjunction of history and theology, but only and also on the basis of a many-sided view of the situation of man in the world, a theme to which natural science and other human sciences also have a right to contribute.

NOTES

1. Bohn, ⁶1848, p.ix.
2. W. H. Dray, *Philosophy of History*, Prentice-Hall 1964, p.4.
3. See *Theologie of History*, ed. P. Gardiner, Free Press of Glencoe, New York, 1959.
4. A. Flew and A. Macintyre (eds), SCM Press 1955.
5. SPCK 1960.
6. SCM Press 1967.
7. Cited in S. M. Daecke, *Teilhard de Chardin und die evangelische Theologie*, Göttingen 1967, p.201.
8. See Daecke, op. cit., pp.202-4.
9. *The Christian Doctrine of Creation and Redemption*, Lutterworth Press 1952, p.35.
10. See, for example, the discussion in J. Dillenberger, *Protestant Thought and Natural Science*, Collins 1961, pp.277f.
11. Stuttgart 1969.
12. Mayer, op. cit., p.287.
13. Ibid.
14. R. Bultmann, *History and Eschatology*, Edinburgh University Press 1957; J. M. Robinson, *A New Quest of the Historical Jesus*, SCM Press 1959; N. Sykes, 'Some Current Conceptions of Historiography and their Significance for Christian Apologetic', *Journal of Theological Studies* L, 1949, pp.24-37.
15. See the discussions in J. Nolte, *Dogma in Geschichte*, Freiburg 1971.
16. W. Windelband, 'Geschichte und Wissenschaft', in *Präludien*, Vol.2, Tübingen ⁵1915, pp.130-60.
17. In *Theories of History*, ed. P. Gardiner, pp.348f.
18. Gardiner, op. cit., p.136.
19. W. H. Dray, *Philosophy of History*, pp.98-112.

V

FAITH, HISTORY AND THE FUTURE OF MAN

IN CHAPTERS I-IV I have explored some of the problems which mark the relations between history and theology. I have considered the constraints which *Historismus* imposes on the theological enterprise and I have pointed to the difficulties which arise for the theologian when he tries to render himself immune to the challenge of *Historismus*. In this chapter I propose to treat directly the question which emerges from this discussion. Does there remain for the theologian any way of reflecting upon human history which is faithful both to the transcendent character of the Christian gospel and to the kind of world disclosed by *Historismus*? I put the question in a positive form because it seems to be clear that so-called secular theology, in its many manifestations, is an evasion of rather than a solution to the problem posed by the language of transcendence. I put the question in a positive form because I take the view that the immense richness of life and thought disclosed by modern historical understanding cannot finally be regarded as other than an enrichment of theological understanding, whatever methodological difficulties it may create. When, however, we recall J. H. Plumb's thesis which I outlined in chapter I, we have in addition to recognize that the theologian's reflection upon human history – if it can be responsibly undertaken – cannot simply be a reflection upon the past. It must directly illuminate the present if it is to serve those who, for complex cultural reasons, no longer experience a living bond with the past. And it must directly illuminate the future, if man's fear about the future is not to paralyse his current ideals and energies. I agree with Ebeling who, in a passage which I quoted in an earlier chapter, spoke of the many unserviceable solutions offered by the last two generations of theologians to the problems which Troeltsch so clearly and so honestly presented. Among those unserviceable solutions we have seen on the one hand Bultmann's impressive and influential proposals, which have called forth since the heyday of his theological activity several variants and internal modifications from his followers, or have been transformed into secular theologies as one or another aspect of his tightly organized scheme has been rejected. We have seen the salvation history of Barth subjected to amendments and apparent improvements, which in fact, as far as their substance is concerned, only reiterate the claims of those theologies of revelation which Troeltsch so critically subjected to the canons of *Historismus*. All the reactions and counter-reactions to the Barthian impulse ultimately founder on biblicistic exegesis and an unwarranted claim to immunity from historical criticism. In general I would consider that the 'theology of history' since Troeltsch has done little to respond positively to the challenges which he put forward. Much of this theology has been defensive in character. In particular it has, to no small extent, ignored his contention that theology must primarily be a living, contemporaneous discipline. In fact many of the Protestant theologians have persisted, in one way or another, in treating theology first and foremost in terms of the bringing of the past into the present. This procedure, so dependent upon Lutheran principles, continually meets the difficulties posed by Troeltsch's historicist triad of correlation, analogy and criticism.

In this chapter I cannot hope to do more than suggest a few guidelines which may help us to steer between the

Scylla of anti-historical existentialism and the Charybdis of unhistorical supernaturalism, in the modest expectation that others may find a few threads to draw into a fuller and more persuasive network of theological understanding. In order to test out some of the contemporary possibilities of a 'theology of history', in the light of *Historismus*, I propose to concentrate upon a single but central topic and I want to experiment with a certain method in relation to this theme.

The theme which I wish to consider is admirably presented by Frank E. Manuel in his *Shapes of Philosophical History*. He writes: 'And yet, much to my amazement, I have found that beneath the surface [of the work of four different groups of philosophical theologians] there is a consensus, albeit an uneasy one, among a substantial body of twentieth-century writers who have examined the historical process in its totality and have ventured to predict its future. They are agreed that the next stage either must or is likely to entail a spiritualization of mankind and a movement away from the present absorption with power and instinctual existence. Toynbee uses the term "etherialization"; in Teilhard de Chardin's private language it is hominization; the Christian theologians speak in more traditional terms of a recrudescence of religious faith; and Karl Jaspers of a second axial period of spirituality like the age of the prophets, of Buddha, and of Confucius. *Consensus populi* was long ago discarded as a criterion of truth; the consensus of philosophers of history may be an even more dubious witness, but there it stands.'[1]

Not surprisingly, Manuel adopts at first a somewhat sceptical attitude to this thesis. 'As a member of the generation of 1910 I have seen my fill of horror in war and peace. I am no Pangloss, nor Professor Tout-va-bienovitch, that Russian doctor fashioned by Céline's mordant wit. In the midst of universal dread of nuclear annihilation, world-wide social revolution, internecine racial wars, the spectacle of fat-land inhabitants committing suicide by overfeeding and of barren lands incapable of preventing the mass starvation of their hungry, the assurances of the prophets of the new spirituality often seem utopian, even a hollow joke. The victims of the twentieth-century slaughter house refuse to believe it.'[2] But he goes on 'As a skeptic I am reluctant to receive the witness of the heralds of the new spirit, and yet it is pouring in upon me from so many diverse sources and directions that I am on the point of surrendering my belief in the ordinary evidence of the senses. I stand on the verge of accepting the new dispensation.'[3]

Manuel's reluctance to accept the hypothesis which he outlines is understandable. Quite apart from the contrary evidence afforded by the miseries and brutalities of this present world, Manuel could also have appealed to the fact that the ideas of a 'spiritualization' of mankind, of an imminent new age, or of an apocalyptic catastrophe, are not uncommon in past eras of human history. The most obvious explanation seems to be that men, conscious of a gulf between the actuality and ideal of human life, project their hopes on to some mythological or religious scheme which makes life bearable by sustaining hope. The history of man is littered with the remains of such visions, often embraced with great fervour, but which have not apparently been realized in any observable sense. Nevertheless, the spiritualization thesis discussed by Manuel does entail our saying that, whatever may have happened in the past, however frequently hopes may have been dashed, on this occasion there are certain grounds for believing that the next stage in the historical process 'either must or is likely to entail a spiritualization of mankind'. I want to consider whether the Christian theologian should feel obliged to regard such an idea as fanciful or whether he should feel disposed to treat it seriously. I want to ask what kind of evidence would count for the theologian in this respect and along what lines he would develop his argument. Finally, if the idea is at all tenable, I should wish to explore what kind of specifically Christian contributions might be introduced.

In the first place, if we treat seriously Troeltsch's notion of human history as a continuous context of becoming (without thereby implying any teleology), then we must regard as legitimate for a theological handling of this theme some sort of 'appeal to history' – as Henson used the phrase. Although Troeltsch makes full allowance for the emergence of novelty in human history, he affirms that such novelty is always partly continuous with what has gone before. If cultural history is a continuous process of becoming, no event can stand in isolation from this stream. In consequence, the theologian, in order to make any statements about the next stage of the history of mankind, must pay careful attention to previous stages and to the present stage. It would be fundamentally unhistorical to imagine that a new stage could come about which had no connections with what went before. So Troeltsch would bid us consider the impulses in that previous history which might be 'brought through' into present and future circumstances.

In the second place, *Historismus*, by its assertion about the connectedness of history, disallows the view that a new stage for mankind could come about as the result of a pure, unmediated act of God imposing itself upon human history from without. I should also conclude that an act of this kind is also disallowed by our understanding of the physical world. I am not arguing that the physical world is so constituted as to be closed to divine influence, only that such an influence would somehow have to be exercised in and through that physical world and could not be extrinsic in character. This rejection of an extrinsicist understanding of God's action is so crucial for my subsequent argument that I shall develop it in greater detail.

It is now widely accepted (and I should myself wish to accept) that the world disclosed by the human and the non-human sciences neither requires nor permits the postulation of extrinsic unmediated divine action. In consequence, the theologian is obliged to say that God has so ordered things as to allow to the world a long, independent and complicated history of self-creation issuing both in 'failure' and 'success'. This is not to suggest that we can derive from the natural order an explanation of why there is something rather than nothing. Nor does it mean that God is to be conceived of as an absentee landlord. It simply means that, in formulating any understanding of the natural order, we must side with those theories which are inherently disposed to allow fully for the contingent character of that natural order. Likewise, in viewing the phenomenon of cultural history, the theologian must take full account of man's growing experience of himself as relatively autonomous. We are reminded of Bonhoeffer's remark that: 'The movement that began about the thirteenth century (I'm not going to get involved in any argument about the exact date) towards the autonomy of man (in which I should include the discovery of the laws by which the world lives and deals with itself in science, social and political matters, art, ethics, and religion) has in our time reached an undoubted completion. Man has learned to deal with himself in all questions of importance without recourse to the "working hypothesis" called "God". In questions of science, art, and ethics this has become an understood thing at which one now hardly dares to tilt.'[4] A similar point is made by Ebeling when he speaks of the 'fundamental change never again to be unmade which came over the self-evident assumptions with the dawn of the modern age'.[5] This change implies a restriction, namely the 'elimination of all metaphysical statements from the realm of the self-evident', and an extension, namely the 'relative autonomy of science and of social life'. 'It is a legitimate self-evident assumption of the modern age, never again to be unmade, that neither the church nor any world-view that supposes itself absolute may impugn the relative autonomy of science and of social life.'[6] The theological consequence of this position is quite clear, even if it is not always clearly recognized in theological practice. We may in no wise speak of God's action so as to undermine or remove this autonomy. Instead, God's action must be construed as alongside and in relation to this autonomy. In other words, this relative autonomy of history and of the world points directly to a positive theological claim, namely that God in his creative purpose has ordered things at an ontological distance from himself – a distance which must continually be borne in mind in all our talk about the character of God's relationship with the world. The main alternative interpretation consists in supposing that the history of man's discovery of the relative autonomy of the world of nature and of historical life is one massive, accelerating and cumulative *aversio a Deo* in which the natural order itself is somehow implicated. I can only regard this interpretation as theologically absurd. It construes as undifferentiated failure all that is entailed in the slow, painful and chequered emergence of man as a thinking, moral being out of a long evolutionary history.

The theologian is therefore bound to reject the kind of salvation history that ignores human autonomy and historicality in the world. On the other hand, the theologian cannot accept autonomy as an exhaustive account of worldly and human reality; this would render him dumb. As I have already suggested in chapter IV, the only positive way forward lies with the elaboration of a dialectical account of God's relationship with the world. Such a dialectical account creates difficulties for the theologian inasmuch as his subject-matter becomes less precise and therefore less easily manageable. But the dialectical approach provides a fruitful means by which we might grasp the significance of the great monuments in the theological tradition. Much of the debate in that tradition centres upon the justification of extreme positions. Is God sovereign or is man free? Is Jesus Christ more like man or more like God? Is the atonement a subjective or an objective event? Is the church to be regarded as primarily a sociological or a theological reality?

One-sided answers to questions such as these have been freely canvassed in the Christian tradition, but their difficulties are widely appreciated. For either they exalt human autonomy to the point where theological talk becomes redundant or they claim an absolute divine initiative which sits uneasily alongside man's experience of autonomy. But it is not enough to say that, by virtue of these difficulties, we should adopt a middle position. A middle position tends to leave us with a compromise between extremes, a static mode of description. The dialectical theory of the relationship between God and man causes us, however, to look afresh at this doctrinal deposit in all its variety.

I take therefore as an axiom that theological discourse has for its subject-matter the dialectical divine-human relationship. It is not concerned with divine or human aspects of this relationship which may be abstracted and examined separately. When therefore the theologian speaks of human autonomy and divine action, he has these in mind as features of this divine-human relationship. By analogy with inter-human relationships, we should think of the divine-human relationship not as a steady fixed pattern but rather as a complex dialectical interplay of closeness and estrangement, question and response, gain and loss, initiative and withdrawal. This dialectical scheme in turn makes us cautious of treating human autonomy and divine action in static, fixed categories. On the dialectical pattern we would not suppose that God's action is always the same or that it always functions in the same way. Similarly, human autonomy is a complex phenomenon. On the one hand we acknowledge that many factors restrict man's free exercise of autonomy; but on the other hand human beings frequently recognize an unconditional element within their experience of autonomy. On this view of autonomy, God's action would be seen as that of a transcendent power in both initiative and self-restraint, but always in love, accepting and not accepting, but always engaging with this movement towards an autonomy which is free of constraints and freely open to the unconditional element.

If this dialectical scheme is accepted, we must regard public historical life (in both individual and collective forms) as the *observable* aspect of the divine-human relationship. When, therefore, the theologian comes to speak of this divine-human relationship, he will be obliged to consider those movements of public, historical life but without supposing that the totality of that relationship is exhausted by its observable aspects. For the theologian, taking the divine-human relationship as his subject-matter, is bound to seek a way of speaking which captures that relationship as a whole, not simply certain aspects of the relationship viewed from different standpoints.

This dialectical scheme has important consequences when it is applied to the topic under discussion, namely the notion that the next step for mankind must or is likely to entail a spiritualization. If such a spiritualization were to occur, it would be a movement in the history of the divine-human relationship. Thus, on Troeltsch's scheme, we should suppose that its emergence will not be totally discontinuous with the previous history of that relationship. This means in turn that, in inspecting the divine-human relationship in the past and the present, we should expect to find impulses which would relate forwards to a possible spiritualization. So it is in principle right that we should consider the divine-human relationship in its various aspects to see whether such impulses exist and what character they evince. Part of this inspection of the divine-human relationship will, as we saw earlier, refer to public, historical life. Of course it would be wrong to expect clear and unambiguous grounds to emerge in support of the claim that a new stage for mankind is imminent. The evidence that we may discern will be appropriate to the broken, dialectical and shifting character of the relationship. On no count do I wish to argue that there are any grounds which point to the *necessary* emergence of this new stage – whether the necessity be human or divine. If the grounds were such as to imply a necessary emergence at the human level, then we should be destroying the voluntarist character of human life. The divine-human relationship would not then be a personal relationship. If we were to argue for this new stage as of divine necessity, we should be destroying the partnership between divine existence and human autonomy. In both cases it is as if a marriage were to be contracted by one or the other partner in a manner that treated quite arbitrarily the state of the relationship and ignored totally the question of the other's consent.

Up to this point I have argued for an understanding of the divine-human relationship as taking place within the actuality of natural, historical and personal life. When this relationship is given a dialectical character, we can allow both for worldly, human autonomy on the one hand, and for a genuine transcendental divine activity on the other hand.[7] Neither men nor God are alone responsible for the broad movements and changes in this relationship; *the movements and changes are products of the total dialectical relationship.* This crucial point of my argument can be illustrated from a consideration of Joachim de Fiore's theology of history.[8]

Joachim held that the Trinity manifests itself progressively in three successive periods of the history of salvation. These three periods are three steps in the progressive self-realization and self-revelation of the Trinity in the history of mankind. Novel in this conception was the sense in which these three ages were directly related to the concrete course of human history – to the extent that Joachim expected the beginning of the age of the Holy Spirit in AD 1260. Moreover, in true Troeltschean fashion, Joachim saw both continuity and discontinuity in the relationship between one age and the next. The age of the Spirit is a new creation, but it also has an inner continuity with the age of the Son. Impulses in one period point forward to fulfilment in the

next, since the whole process is marked by constant development and continuous re-creation. Here we observe a remark-
ably detailed attempt to set concrete history within a
theological framework, without distorting the concrete
history. Joachim even goes so far as to prophesy about the
history of his own time. The Papacy, which belongs to the
second period, will come to an end with the beginning of
the age of the Spirit. I will make three comments on Joachim's scheme.

1. Though attempting to relate his understanding of God
very closely to the course of human history, Joachim finally
sees God as working in and towards man but not *with* and
alongside man. History is really the story of the self-
realization of God rather than (as my own thesis suggests)
the realization of the divine-human relationship.

2. Because of this, Joachim was able to date the history of
the divine self-realization in an arbitrary way. If he had
really given attention to the divine-human relationship, the
scheme would have had to be presented in much more
flexible terms to allow that the outcome of the process
would at each stage be dependent in part upon the contingencies and autonomies of human, historical life.

3. Notwithstanding, Joachim's scheme deserves to be taken
seriously as nothing less than a theology of history. There is
one kind of 'Marxist' criticism of such religious-social historical figures which affirms their importance at one level
but which dissolves the transcendental claims. On this argument we can say that Joachim's theology of history is a
fiction, but a useful fiction because it inspires ideals and
hopes which others embrace, so bringing about the social
change towards which the original vision pointed.

At one level, then, it may be perfectly proper to claim
that those who adopted Joachim's teachings became 'the
protagonists of the revolution through which ecclesiastical
feudalism in the Middle Ages was overcome',[9] and that Joachim's social utopian ideas actually emerge in the radical

Spiritual Franciscans with remarkable consequences for the Franciscan ideal of poverty. But, on the argument which I am developing in this lecture, I should want to elaborate an actual theology of history, one in which a proper account is taken of human autonomy. Thus the overcoming of feudalism would not simply be the empirical consequence of the prophet's vision, but also an actual historical movement in the history of that divine-human relationship to which the theology of history pointed. In other words theology is seeking to refer to an actual divine-human relationship objectively in process. Clearly such a relationship in its totality is not in fact objectifiable, so that we must on the one hand look for objective signs of this relationship in public, historical life, which cannot be adequately interpreted except in the framework of transcendent myth.

I now return to the question posed by Manuel. I want, in the light of what I have already said, to examine how we might reflect theologically about the idea that there *must be* or *might be* a new stage ahead for humanity in terms of 'spiritualization'. In the first place, it follows from my previous argument that there can in principle be no 'must' about this next stage. If the divine-human relationship possesses the dialectical character which I have suggested, if within this divine-human relationship there is genuine human autonomy (qualified only by suasion and never by coercion), then at the most we can say that the next stage of this divine-human relationship *might* entail a spiritualization of mankind. But is it possible to seize upon concrete features of the divine-human relationship at the present time which might point forward to such a possibility? I find this to be the most difficult part of my argument. It entails our singling out significant features of human historical life in the past and at the present, and then treating such features as signs of the divine-human relationship in its human aspect. These features must subsequently be centrally set within a unified understanding of the divine-human relationship – an understanding to which Christology is crucial. I will suggest several lines of approach.

1. We might point to different stages in the history of human life, e.g. in terms of agricultural, industrial and technological civilizations, observing the ever shorter period of time between these phases. We can argue that this development has been desirable since it provides the only stable and adequate basis for universal human welfare. At the same time we recognize that each successive phase has its dark side. But only in the technological era does the dark side reach truly threatening proportions. For here we encounter the possibility that man will lose control over the system which he has created and so be controlled by it. So we must envisage a way of developing universal human welfare which avoids this loss of control. This might be conceived of in terms of a radical jump towards inwardness, individuality and personal value-systems by which the runaway system can be captured and reharnessed. Thus, in non-religious terms, Kahn and Wiener argue that 'this very power over nature threatens to become a force of nature that is itself out of our control' and that human beings must try to 'moderate Faustian impulses to overpower the environment'. 'What is necessary is an unflagging respect for the world as we find it and for dissent and diversity.' 'Above all, there must be a concern for perpetuating those institutions that protect freedom of human choice.'[10] Here are the beginnings of an argument for a greatly enhanced human consciousness towards the consequences of human actions in the world, a developed self-restraint so powerful that it can bring under control a runaway world.

2. On another line of thought, it could be argued that the rapidly increasing volume of data available to man, with the attendant problems of converting it into information, yields certain alternative prospects. If the need for ordered data is ignored we shall be unable to cope with a complex world-system. If the incidence of ordered data continues,

people will be overwhelmed and withdraw into a cybernetically comatose existence which will also threaten the world-system. Or people will develop in themselves, as they have developed mechanically in the computer, the kind of consciousness which can cope effectively and creatively with the ever-increasing flow of information.

3. We can pursue another line by reflecting upon that contemporary concern about the fate of the environment which reflects both a subjective and an objective crisis for human history. The MIT report on *The Limits to Growth* is one of the first large-scale attempts to apply systems-analysis to the problems surrounding the future of our planet. But in order to embark upon the construction of a world-model, a large number of assumptions must be made which in turn imply value-judgments arrived at from outside the model. There are already signs that the MIT report can and will evoke the construction of an infinite number of counter-models. For modest changes in assumptions lead to quite different world-models. Modest disagreements on the factual data which are to serve as input for the model have the same effect. It is therefore in principle hard to see how a world-model could command universal assent, and therefore doubtful whether a planned and common response to the policies suggested by such a world-model is feasible. If such a response were possible it would presumably entail, in present circumstances, nothing less than massive social organization and control on a world scale. But this prospect too has a certain air of unreality. Without doubt we are moving even more quickly towards the physical limits of growth so that important changes, put in hand now, may take too long in their working-out materially to affect the situation. Against this rational approach, the only alternative seems to be a radically different self-understanding, both individually and collectively, in respect of the needs and values of human life. It could in fact be argued that mondial social control would only work if such a new

understanding were to emerge. 'To deflect man in society
from catastrophe will involve a change in his orientation of
a most radical kind ... This must precede, and indeed in-
form, any change in our social arrangements.'[11] What
appears to be required is not a long process of spiritual/
ethical transformation but a more sudden hierarchical jump.
In this regard, Montefiore suggests that there could be more
difficulty than might be supposed in persuading people to
change their attitudes. He appears to believe that this change
can only be envisaged on a religious basis. 'Not even educa-
tion is sufficient to change long inherited tendencies towards
acquisitiveness and greed. What is needed is something akin
to religious conversion; an emotional shock affecting the
very ground of man's being, in which he finds himself responsible to One whose goodness and grace sustains the cosmos in being; a true perspective in which he sees this world
not as an end in itself but in the perspective of eternity: a
sense of the holiness of all created things, sustained by the
Spirit of God, so that to abuse the created order is to grieve
the Holy Spirit of God himself.'[12] However we view Montefiore's proposal, he clearly brings together the need for a
radical change in self-consciousness with the conditions
required to avoid overshooting, with disastrous consequences, the physical limitations of our planet.

While individual arguments may not appear to carry
much weight, there is far greater force in the cumulative
effect of countless possible lines of argument that man is
reaching a crisis of decision about his future which cannot
be separated from his self-understanding. From this I should
be prepared to conclude that a strong case can be made out
for the *desirability* that man, at or near this point in history,
should enter a stage of spiritualization. My case depends
upon the combination of many unique and urgent factors.
But none of these lines of argument show that such a stage
is either *inevitable* or *likely*. Since I have already argued
that, on theological grounds, the idea of inevitability must

be discounted, I confine myself to asking whether there is at present any evidence of *likelihood*. What could count as evidence in this respect? One possibility would be to argue (on Troeltsch's theory of development) that already we can discern impulses of such a spiritualization. The difficulty about this kind of argument is that alongside what may be regarded as spiritualizing impulses, there are also countless impulses of a totally different kind. Notwithstanding, it is reasonable to suppose that the growth of individuals and groups in the direction of spiritualization and away from the attitudes and values which have contributed to our present crisis, would count as evidence that spiritualization was to some extent likely. Certainly if no such individuals or groups existed, we might well want to say that spirituality was a less likely prospect. But for this argument to carry much weight, we should somehow have to show that spiritualization, rather than something else, was being fostered. This is difficult to demonstrate, since spiritual-ization seems to involve some measure of disengagement and of a hidden life. It may, however, be possible to relate many significant signs of interiorization of values in society to this theme of spiritualization. Again, when individual examples are cited the case looks perilously weak. But when examples are taken cumulatively they look more impressive. In this context I have in mind certain kinds of revolutionary movements, community movements, environmental move-ments, radical educational experiments, etc. alongside the decay of long-standing institutions in law, finance, educa-tion, medicine, church, etc. I have to admit that con-siderable difficulties are created for this kind of argument by the ambiguous and ephemeral character of these pheno-mena.

I have now reached the point of claiming that there are grounds, taken cumulatively, which suggest that for the next stage in the history of mankind to be one of 'spiritual-ization' is both subjectively and objectively *desirable*, and

subjectively and objectively *likely* (even though its likelihood is only slight). I now want to enter the last stage of
my discussion by setting this theme of spiritualization in
the context of the dialectical divine-human relationship,
thereby viewing it from the theological standpoint too. For
this to be possible, we require concrete signs of the divine
partnership in this divine-human relationship. In this respect
the Christian theologian feels obliged to turn principally
to the life and destiny of Jesus Christ, as to some extent
moulded by the antecedent histories of the communities of
Israel, and as interpreted and developed by the early Christian and successive Christian communities.

The Christian theologian turns to Jesus Christ because the
Christian church, in its experience, has there found the
exemplary and decisive sign of the dialectical divine-human
relationship. In classical definitions, for example, the church
came to express this relationship, as experienced in Jesus
Christ, in paradoxical terms of the autonomy of the Man
and of the autonomy of God; the self-giving and obedience
of the Man and the self-giving and condescension of God;
and the union and distinction of the Man and God. The
classical definitions reveal, however, the difficulty (indeed
the impossibility) of capturing in static language and sequen-
tial syntax what is a living, dialectical relationship. In consequence, when we might hope for a unified picture of that
dialectical relationship in its ceaseless, complex interplay
and dynamic, we are in fact left with what must inevitably
look like the fixed and stylized personal attributes of a God-
man.

What is the connection between that dialectical divine-
human relationship which is as old and as universal as man's
history and even pre-history, and that decisive divine-human
relationship which is experienced by the church in Jesus
Christ?[13] For the God who is in decisive dialectical partnership with Jesus is the same God who is in dialectical partnership with man in his autonomy and historicality. Moreover,

both relationships belong to worldly historical existence. To attempt an answer to this crucial question we can say : the God-Jesus relationship becomes a historical reality in the world shaping our networks of relationships, understandings and movements of history. The characteristics of this God–Jesus relationship (which I shall consider in a moment) help to elucidate the hidden character of the universal divine-human relationship, help in particular to point to the style of human partnership in that relationship which can be responsive to the divine partnership. So the Christian experience of the God-Jesus relationship not only illustrates and exemplifies the universal divine-human relationship, but illuminates it to expose the kind of partnership which God exercises and the kind of partnership which will be a creative human response. But in no sense does the God-Jesus relationship dictate to, or control in advance, the universal divine-human relationship. But when a man lives out his part in the divine-human relationship in the dynamics of the relationship between God and Jesus, the total divine-human relationship must undergo change. So the dialectical relationship between God and Jesus embarks upon a course through history in which it becomes intertwined with the universal divine-human relationship.

On this view we can see that the theologian is not *principally* concerned with the events of Galilee and Jerusalem as these are remembered and interpreted. The theologian is above all concerned with the historical actuality of the divine-human relationship at successive points in history, and especially in his own present age. But the *method* which the theologian employs to this end certainly *includes* (much as Henson described it) an appeal to the historical source of the tradition, as well as the history of the tradition, and to the history of the world, all of which image the divine-human relationship in its complex, dialectical structure.

From reflection upon the God-Jesus relationship, the theo-

logian reaches certain conclusions about the self-emptying
love of God; about God's purpose to preserve the autonomy
of Jesus through death; about the work of Jesus to create
new relationships, new states of being (forgiveness, etc.) by
a non-coercive ministry; and about the formation and extension of a new community in the power of the God-Jesus
relationship which is constructed by inner bonds and where
all are one in Christ. If these marks of the God-Jesus relationship are universalized into the possibilities of the human-
divine relationship, then we may suppose that God calls
man both to the building-up of the world through the
exercise of maturity and to the spiritual transformation
which is the condition of that maturity. If we are correct in
saying, from without, that mankind faces a mondial crisis,
then the next stage of the history of the divine-human relationship may be considered in terms of a simultaneous divine
persuasion of man towards the fullest assumption of responsibility and towards a mutual human self-giving for the
creation of new relationships and new states of consciousness
which will support and enable that assumption of responsibility. Again this mode of argument does not lead to the
conclusion that a stage of mankind's spiritualization is likely
in any empirical sense. Rather it suggests that if human beings
make themselves more transparent to God by responding to
the call to responsibility in extensive and intensive self-giving,
and in the formation of a catholic community, then mankind
may face the surprise of a spiritualization issuing in a transformed understanding of autonomy and of what it means
to live in dialectical relationship with a God of pure, un-
bounded, self-giving love – but a relationship whose story
would still not be complete.

Thus, against all theological enterprises which seek to
repeat 'earlier constellations of thought', which try to bring
the past into the present, we must continually struggle for
the elaboration of a theological method which is appropriate to both transcendence and to historical existence. In

words of Gerhard Sauter, at the end of an impressive and critical review of theological methodology in *Theologie als Wissenschaft*, we urgently need 'the growth of theological knowledge which is an advance in the pneumatological knowledge of man and of the world'.[14] Only in this way can theology (as Troeltsch always hoped) help modern man 'to break out of the limit of his own cultural forms' and so be open to the 'richness and complexity that the future holds for multi-dimensional man' (E. Cousins). Only in this way can faith, history and man's future come together in an organic and fruitful unity. So for the theologian there is always an appeal to history – the history, past, present and future of the continuous divine-human relationship in the world. To explore the past moments of that relationship is to disclose living and concrete images which help us to identify and trust the reality of that relationship hidden in the present, and help us to learn how to bear creatively the full burden of the new order of divine-human life which is waiting to be born.

NOTES

1. George Allen and Unwin 1965, p.159.
2. Op. cit., pp.161f.
3. Ibid., p.162.
4. Dietrich Bonhoeffer, *Letters and Papers from Prison*, The Enlarged Edition, ed. Eberhard Bethge, SCM Press 1971, p.325 (8 June 1944).
5. G. Ebeling, *Word and Faith*, SCM Press 1963, pp.44f.
6. Op. cit., p.45.
7. I have argued elsewhere that for this reason 'dogmatic' and 'contextual' tendencies in theology must be regarded as complementary. See my 'Dogmatic or Contextual Theology?', in *Study Encounter* VIII, 1972.
8. See E. Benz, *Evolution and Christian Hope*, Victor Gollancz 1967, pp.35-48.
9. Op. cit., p.36.

10. H. Kahn and A. J. Wiener, *The Year 2000*, Collier-Macmillan 1967, pp.412f.

11. M. Sloss, in 'A Symposium on the Blueprint for Survival', *The Teilhard Review* VII, 1972, p.63.

12. H. Montefiore, op. cit., p.56.

13. I have no more than outlined an approach to Christology in this context since I have dealt much more fully with the theme in my 1973 Pollok Lectures on 'The Cosmic Christ and the Historical Jesus: a Reappraisal', delivered at the Atlantic School of Theology in Halifax, Nova Scotia.

14. Munich 1971, p.71.

INDEX